Touring Guide of
PAFOS

Written by

George Karouzis
Geographer-Travel Writter

&

Christina G. Karouzis
Geographer-Cartographer

Center of Studies, Research & Publications
SELAS LTD

Text: *George & Christina G. Karouzis*

Photographs: *G. Karouzis, J. Lambrou*

Maps: *Christina G. Karouzis*

Fourth Revised Edition 2008

ISBN 978-9963-566-95-2

CONTENTS

INTRODUCTION

This comprehensive and richly illustrated touring guide of Pafos aims at acquainting the tourist with the varied and interesting physical and cultural features of Pafos town and Pafos district.

Pafos, with its mountains, hills and coastal plain, its pine-clad forests, its laced and unspoilt beaches, its basilicas, monasteries, castles and medieval churches, Aphrodite's Rock (Petra tou Romiou), the sanctuary of Aphrodite (Kouklia), the mosaics considered to be the finest in the Eastern Mediterranean, the impressive gorge of Avakas and the still pristine Akamas area, constitutes an attractive and fascinating district for the tourist, foreign and local.

The tourists will find in this touring guide, apart from the most significant monuments of Pafos town itself, a detailed description of each village and each place of interest of Pafos district. Moreover, the guide affords a general account of the physical setting, the economic aspects, the historical background and the population data of the district.

We are confident that in the end the foreign visitor will be fascinated by the wealth of historical, physical, cultural and economic features of Pafos district. After all, the antiquities of Pafos are incluted in the official UNESCO World Cultural Heritage list.

The difficult task of preparing this guide was undertaken by George Karouzis, a leading and experienced travel-writer, assisted by Christina G. Karouzis, a geographer-cartographer. Both have written many books and touring guides on Cyprus, or have compiled and designed maps and plans of the island.

SELAS
Center of Studies, Research and Publications

Key to Maps

Motorway		Picnic area		
Motorway junctions		Restaurant		
Main road with road number		Place of interest		
Secondary road		Hospital		
Non-asphalted road		Functioning monastery		
Pedestrian way		Important church		
One way road		Archaeological site and monument		
UK Sovereign Base boundary		Castle-Fort		
District Boundary		Museum		
Limit of area under turkish occupation		Youth hostel		
Airport-Airfield		Golf		
Ferry route		Bank		
Dam		Mine		
Salt lake		Lighthouse		
Beach		Forest station		
The European Blue Flag		Petrol station		
Marina		Nature Trail		
Tourist information office				
Public Organised Beach (C.T.O.)				
Waterskiing				
Fishing				
Hotel				
Hotel apartment				
Camping				

Population

- Municipality
- >2000 inhabitants
- 501 - 2000 inh.
- 251 - 500 inh.
- 0 - 250 inh.
- Abandoned settlements

Height in metres

0	200	600	1000	1600	2000

GENERAL BACKGROUND

☐ PHYSICAL SETTING

Pafos district, situated in the western part of Cyprus, occupies an area of 1395,9 sq km which constitutes about 15,1% of the total area of the island. Its eastern administrative boundaries are Nicosia to the north and Limassol to the south. Its coastal area is characterised by gulfs and coves, capes and points, beaches and tiny isles. Pafos district could be divided into three broad morphological regions: (a) the coastal plain, lying mainly below 200 metres, (b) the hilly area extending from the plain up to the igneous rocks of Pafos forest and (c) the mountainous region, lying mainly on the igneous rocks of the Pafos Forest.

(a) The coastal plain

The coastal plain of Pafos is subdivided into the plain of Pafos and the plain of Chrysochou.

(i) The coastal plain of Pafos

It consists of a narrow coastal strip of land

extending from Petra tou Romiou, close to the Pafos-Limassol administrative boundaries, up to the tiny settlement of St George (Pegeia). The length of the plain is about 45 km, while its width varies, though it does not exceed 8 km. The plain extends even beyond St George, up to the Akamas peninsula, though mixed with forest and rocky surfaces.

The main features of the plain are the marine and river terraces with a gentle slope towards the sea. The traveller along the coastal plain can observe the marine terraces ending up in cliffs facing the sea. At Geroskipou as many as three terraces can be observed. The plain lies mainly on recent alluvium and terrace deposits. The main rivers that traverse the plain, originating mostly in the igneous massif of Troodos, are from south-east to west the following: Chapotami, Diarizos, Xeros, Ezousa and Mavrokolympos.

The coastal plain of Pafos is very fertile, currently irrigated by the Pafos Irrigation Project. As it is obvious, it is intensely

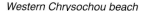

Western Chrysochou beach

cultivated with citrus, vegetables, fruit-trees, potatoes, bananas, table grapes, avocados and peanuts.

(ii) The Chrysochou coastal plain

The coastal plain of Chrysochou extends east and west of Polis, including part of the narrow Chrysochou valley to the south. As in the case of Pafos coastal plain, it consists of marine and river terraces, covered with alluvium and terrace deposits of the Holocene and Pleistocene geological periods. It is irrigated by the Evretou dam as well as by smaller dams in Argaka-Makounta, Agia Marina and Pomos. It is intensely cultivated with fruit-trees, citrus, vegetables and a few banana plants.

(b) The hilly region

It extends from the coastal plain in the south, west and north towards the Troodos complex, where igneous rocks predominate. This is a predominantly dry-fed farming region with carob, olive, almond trees, cereals, legumes and vineyards. The vine-growing villages of Pafos fall within this region, made up of chalks, marls and chalky marls.

From the morphological point of view, it is an undulating country with rounded chalky topography and white lime soils dissected by streams originated in the Troodos massif and adjusted to a radial pattern of drainage.

The topography is rugged, particularly where hard limestones are encountered. Carst phenomena with magnificent stalactites and stalagmites have recently been disclosed in Neo Chorio. In some cases rejuvenation of the river system and downcutting of the valleys has set up a number of deep, steep-sided valleys, ravines and particularly gorges, as in the case of Avakas, west of Arodes. Where

Mamonia Complex formations are present, apart from landslides, there are huge blocks of rocks standing on their own and constituting conspicuous features on the landscape, as in the case of Ineia, Drouseia, Arodes, Nata, Pentalia etc.

The rainfall in the hilly region varies from 500 to 700 mm, while the garrigue scrub vegatation includes species like lentisk, thyme, caper as well as other aromatic plants.

Within the hilly region is included the Akamas forest with its scrub vegatation, composed mainly of junipers and pine-trees. The Akamas forest land, uninhabited for a number of centuries, constitutes a microregion on the grounds of its land use, history, geomorphology and cultural features.

(c) The mountainous region

The region coincides with the igneous Troodos massif (or the Pafos forest), where diabase and lavas predominate. As is obvious, the hard, resistant rocks give rise to a harsh and rugged scenery with deep, steep-sided valleys and ravines as well as abrupt, sometimes vertical slopes. Chestnut lavas, on the other hand, being relatively soft rocks, give rise to gentle, rounded hills.

The radial drainage pattern, developed on Troodos, is clearly exhibited by rivers and streams flowing, south-west, west and north-west.

Rainfall is relatively high ranging from about 750 mm to 900 mm in the Pafos forest.

Some of the best forests of Cyprus, like the Pafos forest with its moufflon, particularly in the Stavros tis Psokas area, are found in this region. The main forest

Cedar trees (Cedar Valley)

trees are the wild pine *(Pinus brutia),* and the cedar trees, *(Cedrus brevifolia)* which is an endemic species present in the Cedar Valley, Tripylos and other places. Among the shrubs is the golden oak *(Quercus alnifolia),* the strawberry shrub *(Arbutus unedo)* and the rockrose *(Cistus).* No doubt, the mountain valleys carry hardwood species, like plane, alder and maple trees. In Orites and Randi, gorse, thyme, wild carobs and olives are dominant. Scrub vegetation known as maquis, mainly developed on siliceous soils, includes plants like rose laurel, arbutus, myrtle, rosemary etc.

Climate

The climate of Pafos district varies according to its morphological regions. The average rainfall of the coastal plain is relatively low, ranging between 430 mm and 500 mm, falling mainly during the winter months, with no rainfall or very negligible rainfall in the summer months.

In Pafos town, for instance, the total annual rainfall is 428 mm with 271 mm falling during Dec-Jan-Febr period, 67 mm in March, April, May, 5 mm in Jun, Jul, Aug, Sept, and 85 mm in Oct, Nov. In Polis (Chrysochou) the total annual rainfall is 474 mm, falling mainly in January (95 mm), February (70 mm), March (61 mm), Nov (64 mm) and December (100 mm). Four summer months (Jun, Jul, Aug, Sept) experience only 6 mm of rainfall.

In the hilly areas the average rainfall ranges between 500 and 750 mm, falling mainly in the winter months with occasional or some rainfall in the summer months.

In the mountainous villages rainfall ranges

between 750 mm and 850 mm with some rainfall in the summer months.

Temperature varies also according to relief. In Pafos town, 10m above sea level, the mean daily temperature for Jan is 13,1°C and for August 26,4°C. Polis experiences 11,8°C in January and 26,5°C in August, Kathikas, 650 m above sea level, lying in the hilly region, experiences a mean daily temperature of 8,3°C in January and 24,3°C in August, while Stavros tis Psokas, a mountainous settlement, 790 metres a.s.l., has a mean daily temperature of 7,2°C in January and 25,2°C in August.

July relative humidity for Pafos is 66% (1 p.m.), for Polis 51%, for Kathikas 49% and for Stavros tis Psokas 36%. Relative humidity for Stavros is, however, high in winter, reaching 83% (8 a.m.) in January.

Polis experiences 4,3 days ground frost per year (mainly in the Dec-March period) while Pafos experiences 8,6 days (mainly in the Nov-April period.)

Pafos town and Pafos coastal plain, which attract a large number of tourists, experience 5,9 hours sunshine duration in February 10,9 in May, 12,3 in July and 8,5 in Oct.

Pafos as a whole experiences relatively high sea temperatures ranging from 15,5°C in February to 19,2°C in May and 25,9°C in August.

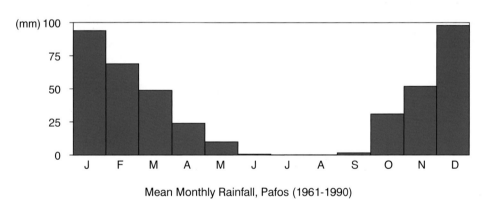

Mean Monthly Rainfall, Pafos (1961-1990)

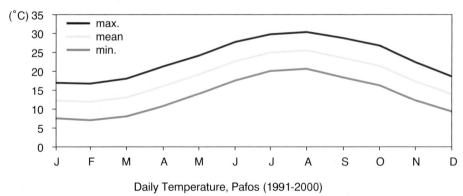

Daily Temperature, Pafos (1991-2000)

Pafos Beaches

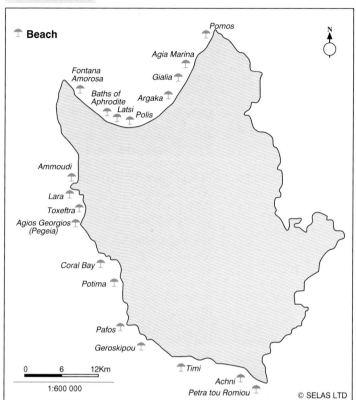

⊤ **Beach**

SEA TEMPERATURE	
Month	(˚C)
Jan.	16,0
Feb.	15,8
Mar.	16,7
April	18,1
May	20,2
June	22,7
July	25,1
Aug.	26,3
Sep.	26,1
Oct.	23,9
Nov.	21,0
Dec.	18,3

© SELAS LTD

PAFOS BEACHES

Petra tou Romiou
Achni
Timi
Geroskipou (Municipal Beach Ⓟ)
Pafos (Pachyammos Ⓟ, Vrysoudia A Ⓟ, Vrysoudia B Ⓟ, Alykes Ⓟ, Municipal Baths Ⓟ, Faros Beach Ⓟ)
Potima
Coral Bay Ⓟ
Agios Georgios (Pegeia)
Pegeia (Laourou Ⓟ)
Toxeftra
Lara
Ammoudi

Geranisos
Fontana Amorosa
Baths of Aphrodite
Western Gulf of Chrysochou
Latsi
Polis (Municipal Beach Ⓟ, Dasoudi Ⓟ)
Eastern Gulf of Chrysochou (Argaka, Gialia etc)
Pomos
Pachyammos (in Nicosia district)

Ⓟ **Beaches awarded the Blue Flag**
The Blue Flag is annually awarded to Beaches that comply with a list of criteria (water quality, environmental education and information to beach area management and safety)

☐ HISTORICAL BACKGROUND

Prehistoric period

Though no settlement of the Neolithic period (7500-3900 B.C.) has, so far, been unearthed in the Pafos district, nevertheless subsequent historical periods are adequately represented. It has, however, been written that at the locality "Agios Mamas" of Androlikou, a neolithic settlement has been located.

Chalcolithic settlements (3900-2500 B.C.) are represented by Lempa, Kisonerga and Souskiou. a copper chisel from Lempa, a copper spiral from Souskiou and a copper hook from Kisonerga justify the name "Chalcolithic", which means stone-copper age.

The Bronze age (2500-1050 B.C.) subdivided into Early (2500-1900 B.C.), Middle (1900-1650 B.C.) and Late (1650-1050 B.C.) is adequately represented. At Kisonerga and Gialia, cemeteries of the Early Bronze Age have been located, while the Middle Bronze Age is represented by the extensive cemetery of Pano Arodes. Palaepafos (Kouklia) belongs to the Late Bronze Age, while the settlement of Maa-Palaiokastro dates back to the 12th century B.C.

Early historic times

The Cypro-Geometric period (1050-750 B.C.) is represented by the cemeteries at "Skales" (Palaepafos) and "Mouttalos" (Pafos), while the Cypro-classical period (475-325 B.C.) is represented by the fortification works of Palaepafos and the cemetery of Mario (Polis).

The Hellenistic period (325-50 B.C.) is among others, perfectly represented by the Tombs of the Kings (Pafos),while the mosaics of Pafos, the Odeion, Asklepieion and the Agora belong to the Roman period (50 B.C.-330 A.D.)

Lempa chalcolithic settlement

Old wine press (Pano Arodes)

Building 2

Chronological Table of the Main Prehistoric and Historic Periods of Cyprus		
Neolithic		7500-3900 B.C.
Chalcolithic		3900-2500 B.C.
Early Bronze Age		2500-1900 B.C.
	First contacts with the Aegean and the Middle East 2000 B.C.	
Middle Bronze Age		1900-1650 B.C.
Late Bronze Age		1650-1050 B.C.
	Myceneans	*1400 B.C.*
Iron Age		about 1050 B.C.
Geometric		1050-750 B.C.
	Phoenicians at Kition	*9th c.B.C.*
Archaic		750-475 B.C.
	(i) Assyrians	*673-669 B.C.*
	(ii) Egyptians	*560-545 B.C.*
	(iii) Persians	*545-332 B.C.*
Classical		475-325 B.C.
Hellenistic		325-50 B.C.
Roman		50 B.C.-330 A.D.
Byzantine		330-1191 A.D.
Cyprus under Richard Lionheart		1191 A.D.
Frankish		1192-1489 A.D.
Venetian		1489-1571 A.D.
Turkish		1571-1878 A.D.
British		1878-1960 A.D.
Republic of Cyprus		1960+

Churches and Monasteries

Early Christian basilicas are those of Panagia Chrysopolitissa, (4th c.A.D.) Panagia Limeniotissa (5th c.A.D.) and three basilicas at Agios Georgios (Pegeia), 6th c.A.D.

In the 9th century A.D. the five-domed church of Agia Paraskevi, at Geroskipou, was built.

Not many churches have been preserved of the Middle Byzantine period (10th-12th century A.D.). Churches of the 12th century A.D., though destroyed, are preserved at Choulou, at Agios Minas (Neo Chorio) and at the Georgian monastery at Gialia. The first phase of the well-known church of Agioi Kirykos and Ioulitti at Letymvou belongs to this period.

Churches of the 13th c.A.D. are those of Agios Theodosios, (Acheleia), Panagia Chryseleousa (Empa), Panagia Chryseleousa (Chlorakas).

Churches of the Frankish-Venetian period are those of Archangelos and Panagia at Choli, of Agios Nikolaos at Galataria, of Agios Georgios Komanon, of Agios Andronikos (Polis) etc.

Churches of the Turkish period are those of Stavros tis Minthas at Tsada, Agios Savvas tis Karonos, Chrysorrogiatissa, Agios Georgios Nikoxylitis at Drouseia etc.

Architecture

The architecture of the churches and monasteries varies considerably, ranging

Pafos District - Cultural Map

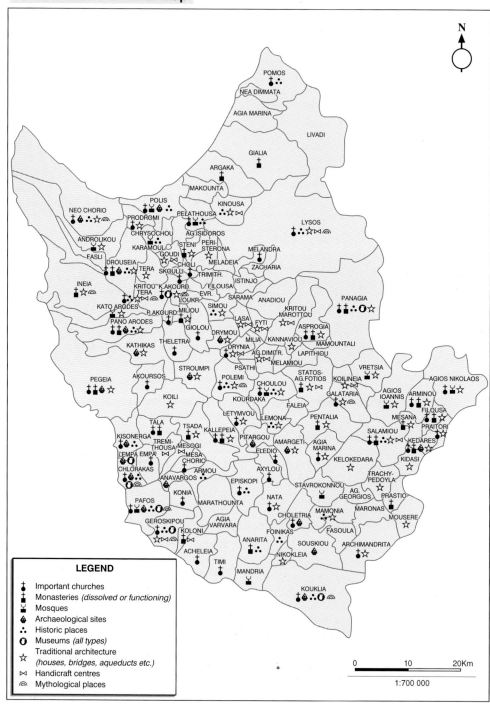

LEGEND

- ✝ Important churches
- ▲ Monasteries *(dissolved or functioning)*
- ⚱ Mosques
- ⬟ Archaeological sites
- ∴ Historic places
- ◉ Museums *(all types)*
- ☆ Traditional architecture *(houses, bridges, aqueducts etc.)*
- ⋈ Handicraft centres
- ◠ Mythological places

0   10   20Km

1:700 000

from the ruined basilicas of the 4th, 5th and 6th century, to the arched churches, like that of Agios Minas at Neo Chorio, the single-aisled churches with dome, like Panagia Chortena (Pelathousa) or Agia Aikaterina (Tala), the cruciform type with dome like that of Agioi Kirykos and Ioulitti (Letymvou) and the three-aisled vaulted church of the monastery of Moni (near Agios Fotios-Statos). Even Gothic relics are still present at a cathedral church at Pafos, where only a part of the wall is preserved, while steep-pitched churches on the mountains are present at Filousa Kelokedaron (Agia Marina and Agios Nikolaos).

Other cultural monuments

Other cultural features, apart from prehistoric and historic antiquities and settlement sites, as well as churches and monasteries, are the castles of Pafos, like the Venetian castle near the harbour and the medieval castle of Saranta Colones. In addition, the visitor can see the medieval baths at Pafos, the manor house and the sugar-mills at Kouklia, the medieval bridges of Skarfos, (Simou), Kelefos and Roudia near Agios Nikolaos and Agios Ioannis villages. In some villages wine presses, belonging to the last century, carved on limestone outcrops in the vineyards are preserved, like the old wine-press at Pano Arodes.

Almost all the villages of Pafos district are recorded on the Venetian maps and are mentioned by medieval chroniclers. Almost all of them were either feuds or royal estates during the Frankish period (12th-15th c.A.D.).

Pafos in Medieval times

Pafos, after all, is the native place of Aphrodite, the Goddess of Love and Beauty. According to tradition, she was born at Petra tou Romiou, while the centre of her worship was at Kouklia, where there was a magnificent temple attracting pilgrims from all over the world. Close to Polis (Chrysochou), according to tradition, she would bathe (Baths of Aphrodite), while at Akamas and in many other places of Pafos she reigned either as Aphrodite or as Rigaina, as she was known in the Middle Ages.

Finally it could be underlined that the numerous archaeological sites and the historic monuments of Pafos are included in the World Cultural Heritage List of UNESCO, since 1980.

☐ ECONOMIC ASPECTS

Until a few years ago, Pafos' economy was entirely based on its primary sector.

Manufacturing and tourism are recent activities.

Mining was, until rery recently, concentrated in the Limni mines, run by the Cyprus Sulphur and Copper Company. The modern works date back to 1882, which continued until 1920. The production of copper began in 1937 and continued until 1979, when the mine was closed after the reserves were exhausted. Besides, copper, gold, silver and sulphur were worked out in the mines. Scoriae (mine waste) appearing in places between Polis-Limni-Kinousa, most probably date back to the Bronze Age and the Roman times. Mining as well as ancillary activities employed a large number of workers from the neighbouring villages.

Agriculture was for a long time the main economic activity of the countryside. It was, however, soon realised that dry-fed crops could not ensure a decent living for

Asprokremmos dam

Tourist complex (Pafos)

the farmers. Efforts were exerted to harness, through dams, the rain water flowing in streams and ending up in the sea. Dams were constructed at Argaka-Makounta, Agia Marina, Mavrokolympos, Pomos, Asprokremmos and Evretou, which encouraged the irrigation of the coastal plains of Pafos and Chrysochou. It is in these two areas that two major irrigation projects were initiated for the irrigation of 5.084 ha and 4.310 ha respectively. Through the increase of irrigable water, large agricultural areas have been planted with vegetables, fruit-trees, table-grapes, citrus, industrial crops and fodder crops.

A new dam, at Arminou, on the upland region of Pafos, has recently been constructed. As it is well known, the Government of Cyprus has been trying to solve the water problem through the storage of natural rain and the desalination of sea water.

It is estimated, that a hectare of irrigable land can give to the farmer ten or fifteen times more income than an equivalent area under dry-fed cultivation. It is worth mentioning that irrigation in the plains was accompanied by land consolidation implementation, including the establishment of a new rural network. Thus, the landscape is modernised with large plots served by access roads while on the sloping terrain artificial terraces have been constructed. Dry-fed crops, still cultivated, are: cereals, olive trees, vines, carob trees, legumes and dry fodder crops.

Animal raising is not well developed in Pafos, as in other districts. However sheep-rearing, goat-raising and dairy

Flower cultivation, Koloni

Traditional houses (Fyti)

cattle are pursued in some villages. With the increase of tourism as well as the stabilization or increase of population in the district, animal husbandry is expected to expand.

Fishing has been encouraged by the extensive coastal area of Pafos, as a result of which four fishing shelters at Pafos, Agios Georgios (Pegeia), Latsi and Pomos have been established. Many Cypriots travel to Pafos for a fish meal. They find the fish tasty, though sometimes it can be rather expensive.

Manufacturing industry is concentrated in the industrial estate of Mesogi and the industrial zone of Anatoliko. Some minor centres are found in relatively large villages. Until the middle of the 1980's Pafos employed only 3,3% of Cyprus industrial workers and possessed only 8,3% of Cyprus industrial units. In fact, industry in the district developed immediately after the 1974 Turkish invasion. Industry in Pafos is light and includes traditional activities (food, tobacco processing, wines, clothing, footwear, furniture and wood) as well as plastic products, metallic products, paper etc.

Pafos together with Limassol are the two main vine producing areas of Cyprus. There is a SODAP winery at Pafos while the KEO winery is no longer operating. Local wineries producing excellent wines, are found at Chrysorrogiatissa monastery (Monte Rogia Winery). The monastery has a very long tradition in wine making, dating back to the year 1760. Currently, it produces around 70.000 bottles a year. Pekris Wines Ltd is a private winery, situated in Pafos and founded in 1986. It currently produces around 30.000 bottles mainly from grapes of Polemi-Panagia area. The Vouni-Panagia Winery, founded in 1987, is a private winery, producing around 100.000 bottles, mainly from the grapes of Panagia village. Kathikas a new vine-producing village.

Handicraft is carried out in some villages since antiquity. Currently, weaving is a prerogative of Fyti and the neighbouring villages. Embroidery carpet-making, basket making and the decoration of kolodja (marrows) are still carried out by a few persons in some villages. At Koloni there are two modern potteries, functioning on an industrial basis, producing traditional pottery products.

Tourism in Pafos is a recent development, initiated by the 1974 Turkish invasion and the occupation of two basic tourist areas of Cyprus, in Famagusta and Kyrenia. No doubt, the particular characteristics of Pafos, sooner or later, would generate the tourism activity experienced in recent years in Cyprus. The climate, the scenery, the coastland, the natural vegetation, the archaeology and history of Pafos as well as the friendliness of people are factors inducing tourism. The majority of tourists visiting Pafos come from Europe with a small number from other continents. Four tourist areas have already been established in Pafos: (a) Pafos town extending to Geroskipou, south-east, and Chlorakas-Kisonerga to the north. (b) Polis extending to Latsi and Neo Chorio to the west. (c) Coral Bay. (d) Tala. Minor centres are being developed in Drouseia, Agios Georgios (Pegeia) and Tsada.

Pafos is currently (figures of 2006) the leading tourism centre of Cyprus with 29.058 beds, followed by Agia Napa (20.935) and Paralimni (16.657). There are 61 hotels 5-1 star, 39 hotel apts, 11 tourist villages, 133 tourist villas, 24 tourist apts and 29 traditional buildings.

In Pafos stay the majority of Britons, Germans, Dutch, Israeli as well as tourists from Belgium and Ireland.

In fact 34%, of all tourists visiting Cyprus prefer Pafos for their holidays. The average length of stay is 10,6 days and the average expenditure per person is € 814.

Trade activities are limited, centered along a few commercial roads as well as along the coastal road of the tourist area of Pafos. Large superstores have recently appeared in a few places of Pafos town. The persons employed on commerce are steadily increasing as well. However, there is a relatively large range of commercial units extending from restaurants to retail shops.

DAMS

Agia Marina
Argaka-Makounta
Arminou
Asprokremmos
Evretou
Mavrokolympos
Pomos

FISHING SHELTERS

Agios Georgios (Pegeia)
Latsi
Pafos
Pomos

HANDICRAFT

Weaving: Fyti, Lasa, Kritou Marottou, Drynia, Agios Dimitrianos etc.
Embroidery: Goudi, Fyti, Statos, Lysos (all old centres)
Carpet-making: Salamiou, Koilineia, Trimithousa.
Basket-making: Mesogi
Chair-making: Kinousa
Pottery: Koloni (Modern factories producing, among others, traditional pottery products).

Gathering grapes

VINES AND WINES OF CYPRUS

Cyprus was famous for its grapes and wines since ancient times. Most probably the cultivation of grapes started in the 2nd millenium B.C., if not earlier. Though there is no direct evidence for the production of wines in ancient Cyprus, indirect evidence might prove that wine was produced in the late bronze age. During the Roman times the mosaics of Kato Pafos, dating back to the 3rd century A.D., illustrate how important wine drinking was in daily life. In the Middle Ages Cyprus was famous for its wines. The Knights Templar, who established their Grand Commandery at Kolossi, owned land in Limassol, Koilani, Avdimou and Pafos. They produced their own wine which was later known as the "Vin de Commanderie".

Etienne de Lusignan (1580) praises the wines of Cyprus as "the best in the world". It is also said, though not documented, that the sweet Cyprus wine was the main inducement for the conquest of Cyprus by the Turkish Sultan Selim II in 1571. Viticulture is still important today and is favoured by the climatic and edaphological conditions of the island. Today 23.500 hectares of vines (21.500 wine grapes and 2.000 table grapes) are under cultivation, with an annual production of 200 million kilogrammes of grapes. Almost one quarter of the agricultural population is engaged in viticulture, which contributes about 7% of the total value of the agricultural production, whilst vine products are one of the main export items of the island. Wine grapes are a dry-fed crop, while table grapes are irrigated. Wine grapes are grown on hilly and semi-hilly areas of the southern and western slopes of Troodos mountains. Table grapes are grown on the irrigated plains of Limassol and Pafos. The wine grapes cultivated are mainly of local varieties (90%): mavro (black) is planted in 73% of the total wine grape area, while xynisteri (white) occupies 14% of the total wine grape area. Other traditional varieties are Malaga (Muscat of Alexandria), Ophthalmo, Maratheftiko, Promara, Spourtico and Kanella. There are also new varieties which do not cover more than 10% of the total wine grape area. Some of the new varieties introduced in Cyprus are Carignan, Grenache, Mataro, Palomilo, Riesling, Malrasia etc. It is not allowed to expand the area planted with vines, whilst replanting has to be made only within the traditional viticultural regions. Within the areas planted with table grapes, sultana, the white seedless variety, occupies 85% of the total table grape area, cardinal 5%, perlette 4% and gold 1%. Sultana, when properly treated gives the large berries known as Thompson Seedless grapes, well known abroad, where they are exported. About 70% of the island's grape production is processed by wineries into wine and other wine products. A variety of wines is made from the various grapes, from dry white and red wines to medium dry and sweet, sherries, brandies and the famous *Commandaria*. This sweet wine was crowned by King Philippe Augustus as "the apostle of wines" in 1223 or even earlier. Soon after it became known as "Commandaria", which was the name of the area where the wine was produced. This area was part of the lands kept by the Order of the Knights Templar who bought the island from Richard Coeur de Lion in 1192 and they sold it soon after to Guy de Lusignan. The Templars built the Kolossi Castle, while in 1210 the Knights of the Order of St John came to Cyprus and they took a neighbouring estate, known as the "Grand Commandery". After the Templars were disbanded their area was taken over by the Knights of St

John, who became in 1307 masters of the whole area around Kolossi and gave the wine the name of "Vin de la Commanderie". Ever since the name of the area is associated with this sweet wine and even its method of production has not changed to this date. Commandaria is the wine with the oldest tradition in the whole world, as far as the method of production and the appellation of origin is concerned. Commandaria is said to be the pioneer of the concept "appellation of origin".

The main wine activity of the island is focused in Limassol with KEO (founded in 1927), LOEL (1943), ETKO (incorporated in 1947) and SODAP (1947). Smaller wineries are found in Koilani (Agia Mavri), Agios Amvrosios (Ecological winery), Statos-Agios Fotios (J. Efstathiou winery), Arsos (Laona winery), Chrysorrogiatissa monastery (Monte Rogia winery), Anogyra (Nikolaides Bros winery), Omodos (Olympus wineries), Pafos (Pekris winery), Panagia (Vouni-Panagia winery) etc. These wineries are open to visitors.

(For more information on wines and grapes, see: Vine Products Commission, "Vines and Wines of Cyprus, 4000 years of tradition", Limassol, 1993).

❑ POPULATION DATA

Pafos, according to the census of 2001, has a total population of 67.432 persons, a figure that represents 9,6% of the population of the free part of Cyprus. The main town of Pafos district, the homonymous capital has a population of 26.530 persons (Pafos Municipality), that is, 40% of the total population of Pafos district. The broader urban area of Pafos has a population of 47.198, that is, 60% of the total population of Pafos. Pafos is the fourth most populous town of Cyprus after Nicosia, Limassol and Larnaka.

There is only one settlement, Geroskipou, which surpasses 5.000 persons apart from Pafos town. Geroskipou has a total population of 5.509 persons, while settlements with a population above 3.000 persons are Empa (3.664) and Chlorakas (3.201). Even settlements between 1000 and 3000 persons are only five: Pegeia (2.362), Polis (1.847), Tala (1.605), Kisonerga (1.404) and Mesogi (1.208).

The main population increases that have been recorded between the last two censuses concern Pafos town, the settlements around Pafos, Polis and the environs of Polis.

Pafos town has grown an account of tourism, industry as well as of being an important service centre for the whole district. Moreover, a number of refugees have settled in Pafos, while currently Pafos' economy attracts a number of Cypriots from other parts of Cyprus as well as from abroad.

Polis, the second service centre of Pafos district, lying in the middle of Chrysochou coastal plain and at the junction of the Chrysochou valley and plain, has stabilized its population. It is, currently, being developed into a tourist centre, apart from its manifold services. The surrounding agricultural land is costantly being improved and irrigated with remunerative crops.

What is alarming is that in 81 settlements of the Pafos district (out of 110 settlements) a decrease-marked or slight-has been recorded the last twenty years. Almost all of these villages lie in the mountainous or hilly part of Pafos district.

Geroskipou settlement

Hilltop rural settlement (Armou)

The hilly and mountainous environment, the dry-fed crops which are not normally remunerative, the lack of natural resources and the absence of employment opportunities have contributed to the exodus of people, attracted mainly by Pafos town as well as Limassol and Nicosia town. However, in the last few years only a few Pafians seek employment outside Pafos district.

Moreover, Pafos has the largest number of abandoned settlements, mainly Turkish Cypriot villages, which have not attracted refugees (after the Turkish invasion of 1974) or other persons.

It is worth mentioning, however, that the mountainous and hilly villages have preserved their traditional architectural character, their old habits, customs and hospitality. Their environment is aestheticaly attractive and picturesque.

Abandoned settlements

Agios Isidoros	Maronas
Agios Merkourios	Meladeia
Agyia	Melamiou
Anadiou	Melandra
Evretou	Mirmikofou
Faleia	Moro Nero
Fasli	Mousere
Foinikas	Paliampela
Istinjo (Kio)	Pera Vasa
Kato Archimandrita	Pitargou
Kato Panagia	Pittokopos
Kidasi	Prastio
Kourdaka	Sarama
Lapithiou	Souskiou
Livadi	Tera
Loukrounou	Trimithousa
Malounta	Vretsia
Mamountali	Zacharia

THE TOWN OF PAFOS

Pafos, a coastal city and capital of the Pafos district, is the westernmost city of Cyprus, centrally situated in the Pafos plain. The Troodos mountain range to the east and the relatively large distances separating Pafos from central and eastern Cyprus, kept Pafos in relative isolation for many years. It is approximately 147 km from Nicosia, 182 from Famagusta (the island's main port prior to 1974), 132 km from Larnaka (next to today's international airport) and 66 km from Limassol, the nearest city.

The city has been known by various names throughout the centuries, such as Nea Pafos, Erythrae, Klavdia, Sevasti, Flavia, Palaea and, recently, Ktima, though in 1971, following a Ministerial Council decision, its name was changed to Pafos.

According to tradition, Pafos was founded by Agapenor, a hero of the Trojan War from Arkadia. The archaeological pick, however, has yet to uncover anything dating from before the 4th century B.C., hence the formulation of the hypothesis

that Pafos was founded by Nikokles, one of her kings.

During the Hellenistic period, the kingdoms of Cyprus, as is well known, were dissolved, and Cyprus was wholly incorporated into the Ptolemaic kingdom. The most significant event of the period is the selection of Pafos as the capital of the island, a fact attributed to the following reasons: its proximity to Alexandria, the seat of the Ptolemies; the safety it offered at the time and the significant and valuable lumber obtained from the Pafos Forest, mainly for the construction of military and merchant ships. It may be that the shrine of Aphrodite at Palaepafos (Kouklia), with the large number of pilgrims and its financial well-being, was taken into account. There can be no doubt that the selection of Pafos as capital of Cyprus brougt about the economic development and cultural progress of the city. It is during this period that impressive edifices and public buildings were erected, while the Tombs of the Kings still constitute one of the

The casle of Pafos before British occupation (engraving)

most impressive remnants of the Ptolemaic period.

During the Roman period Pafos continued as the capital of Cyprus, and a large number of Romans settled there. In 15 B.C., the city was razed by an earthquake, and was rebuilt with the help o Emperor Octavian Augustus. The city, in honour of the emperor, was renamed Augusta, while later, in 22 A.D., as beneficiary of Tiberius Claudius, it was renamed Claudia. In the same way, it was renamed Flavia in honour of Titus Flavius. It is in Pafos that the Apostles Paul and Barnabas preached Christianity in 45 A.D. Sergius Paulus was the first Roman governor to embrace Christianity, and the island itself was the first Roman province with a Christian governor. Remnants of the Roman period are the Pafos mosaics, as well as the pillar at which, according to tradition, the Apostle Paul received 39 lashes.

During the Byzantine period the island, as could be expected, came under the eastern domain, later to become known as the Byzantine Empire. During this period Pafos ceased to be the capital of Cyprus, being replaced by Salamis, an occurrence which deprived Pafos of substantial benefits. Furthermore, the city was struck by strong earthquakes which destroyed its noteworthy buildings. In addition, it is during this period that Pafos was subjected to numerous attacks and raids by the Arabs, especially those of the 7th century A.D. However, it is during the Byzantine period that a number of basilicas were erected, including that of Chrysopolitissa in Kato Pafos, whose dimensions were large for its time. The Pafos fort, aimed primarily at repelling Arab raids, was also built during this period. The fort of Pafos continued its normal operation and it, as well as the port, are mentioned by Saint Neophytos.

Aphrodite of Pafos (Greco-Roman period)
(Photo courtesy of the Dept. of Antiquities)

During the Frankish period the Pafos port was used as a stop for east-west traffic, while the Pafos fort was still considered quite strong. It has not yet been ascertained if, during this same period, there existed another fort, which has since been destroyed. What is mentioned is the existence of a Gothic cathedral, a number of Latin churches and baths. The seat of the Orthodox See was transferred to Arsinoe (Polis Chrysochou), with Pafos becoming the seat of the Latin bishop. The 13th century earthquakes caused serious damages to Pafos, to such an extent that foreign visitors would describe it as "desolate", "destroyed", "a miserable village" etc. During the Frankish period, Ktima, the new name by which Pafos became known, appears, according to Mas Latrie, to have been a royal estate under Acheleia administration. As such, a small royal estate, situated on an elevated marine terrace, possessing a healthy climate, at a distance from the Pafos coastal plain which was subject to the ravages of malaria, Pafos was destined to

Pafos Town - Street Map

MEDITERRANEAN SEA

N

TO CORAL BAY, POLIS

"Tombs of the Kings" Rock-cut tombs

To Arch. Museum

Arch. Museum

AGIOU EFRAIM

KATO PERIVOLION

TAFON TON VASILEON

AGAPINOROS

ANDREA OMIROU

APOSTOLOU PAVLOU

ADAMANTIOU KORAI

ARCHIEPISKOPOU

GREGORIOU AFXENTIOU

GEORGIOU GRIVA DIGENI

CHARALAMPOU MOUSKOU

EVAGORA PALLIKARIDI

KOSTA KANARNAOU

MAKARIOU III

GLADSTONOS

ANAPAFSEOS

MOUSALLAS

MITROPOLITOU NIKODIMOU MYLONA

Municipal Market

Municipal Library

Playing Field

Police Station

Town Hall

Municipal Gardens

Pafos District Court

Pafos Distr. Office

Cy-Airways Offices

Agios Ioannis

Byzantine Museum

Ethnographical Museum

Agios Epifanios

Agios Kendeas

Ag. Theodoros

Bishopric

MARIAS LOIZIDOU

MARTIOU 25

GEORGIOU KANNAS

MAKEDONIAS

SOGNINAS

IREIROU

KORYTSAS

TEPELENIOU

GEORGIOU

ANNIS IOANNIS

BOUMBOULINAS

ANDREA GEROUD

ADONIDOS

ZINONOS KITIEOS

VL. IRAKLEOU

LEONIDOU

EVAGORA

AFRODIZ

PETRIDI MILITIADOU

AFRODITIS

NIKOU ANTONIADI

GALAI OFKOLOU

MOUTALIAKOVRI

SISI MALLIOTOU

P. GEORGIOU

ALEAS ATHINAS

TEGEA

CHRYSANTHEMON

LYSION

VRISIS

EKAVIS

ILIADOS

ELEKTRAS

FRYNIS

NIOVIS

PINELOPIS

PANDORAS

KIKIRIS

SPODON

PTOLEMAIDOS

LEFKADON

PRIAMOU

ALEXANDREIAS

ANDROMACHIS

PANSODA

AMATHOUS

THRAKIS

LAKONIAS

KISSIAS

KALAMATAS

AGRINIOU

KRITIS

EXO IVISIS

GEORGIOU SAVA

PANIKOU PASTID

CHR. ARTEMIOU

APRILIOU 1

ALKIVIADOU

ALKIVIADOU

D. MAVROGENOUS

PANTELIDI

KRANIDIOU

GALA OFKOLOU

ANDREA CHRISTODOULOU

ARIADNIS NIKOLAOU

GALATIAS ZINONOS

GEORGIOU CHRISTODOULOU

MICHAIL KYPRIANOU

G. MICHAIL

G. SAVVA

DIMITRIOU GEORGIOU

IAKOVOU CHRISTODOULOU

TH. ZINONOS

CH. FILIPPIDI

CHRISTOU ARISTODIMOU

SPERANTZA

ANAXAGOROU

AGIOI AVGOUSTINOU

KASSIOU

ALI NASIOU

FEIDIOU

ALVERTOU

ANTIPA

ANANIA

ARION

ARISTARCHOU

GIALOUSAS

VYRONA

IRODOTOU

PYRAMOU

PYRAMOU

KONSTANTINOU KAVAFI

STRATI MYRIVILI

LORENTZOU MAVILI

MAKEDONIAS

AMFITRIONOS

VASSILISSIS VEREKINIS

TILEMACHOU

AIANTOS

EKTOROS

AGINOROS

ANGELOU SIKELIANOU

GEORGIOU SEFERI

PANTELI MICHANIKOU

PAPARRIGOPOULOU

FLEXIS

AGIAS

THEKLAS

LAPITHOU

MORFOU

© SELAS LTD

KATO PAFOS

TO LIMASSOL
NICOSIA

SPYROU KYPRIANOU

Sanctuary of Apollo
Ilatis (Rock-cut)

TAXIARCHON

AGIAS ANNIS

AGIOU ISIDOROU

TASOU MAKROU

AGIOU FOTIOU

AGIOU MEGALOU NOU

SOTIRAKI MARKIDI

DIMITRIOU PASCHALIDI

PASCHALI PASCHALIDI

NIKOLAOU ECONOMOU

POMONOU

KONTONAITOU

DIMITRIOU
KONSTANTINOU

PRIAMOU

LAODIKIAS

DANTOU

AILIAS

DRAMAS

GLYFADAS

MELINAS MERKOURI

KLEIOUS

OTHELLOU

Vrysoudia B

POSEIDONOS

Alykes

Municipal
Beach

0   250m

1:11 000

AGAPINOROS

PARI

ANTIGONIS

PELAPAISIOU

AGISILAOU

AIOU IOU

AGIOU AMVROSIOU

PENTADAKTYLOU

AGIOU MAMANTOS

AGIOU ILARIONOS

PYROGTELOU

IKAROU

AGIOU GAVRIIL

AGIOU
AIGOU
AG. FLENOS

SPYROU KYPRIANOU

DEFKALIONOS

KONSTANTIAS

SMORASIS

Agios
Georgios

Agia Faneromeni

AGAPINOROS

APOLLONOS

NESTOROS

IASONOS

KIKERONOS

DIAGOROU

AISOPOU

APOLLONOS

SOMOTLOU

TEFKROU

Ag. Antonios

AGIAS NAPAS AGIOU ANTONIOU

DIONISOU

ARTEMIDOS
Aquarium

POSEIDONOS

ALKMINIS

LIDAS

SININIS

AGION ANARGYRON

IFAISTOU

KADMOU

Agios
Agapitikos

Rock of
Digenis

Fabrica

Agios
Lamprianos

Agia
Solomoni

Theatre

Agia Marina

AGIOU AGAPITIKOU

ASKLIS FANEROMENIS

PROTAGORA

AGAMEMNONOS

MINOOU

PAPA SAVOUTS

ATREOS

AGIOU PAVLOU

Agia Kyriaki

Agios
Georgios

Frankish
Baths

St Paul's
Pillar

KYTINAMNISTRAS

Theoskepasti

THEOSKEPASTIS

APOSTOLOU PAVLOU

PROMITHEOS

PARMENIONOS

ELEFTHERIOU CHANDRINOU

AFON TON VASILEON

AGIOU LAMPRIANOU

PLOUTARCHOU

Garrison's camp

ONISILOU

AGMS
SOLOMONIS

AGIAS KYRIAKIS

STILIS AGIOU PAVLOU

PENEIAS

ARC. Chrysopolitissa
Basilica

AGIAS GALATANIS

Latin Cathedral

SARANTA KOLONON

KYRIAKOU NIKOLAOU

Saranta Kolones

Archaeological Park

Walls (north-west gate)

(Probable acropolis)

Agora

Odeion

Asklepieion

House of Dionysus
(Mosaics)

House of Aion
(Mosaics)

House of Theseus
(Mosaics)

House of Orfeus
(Mosaics)

Limeniotissa
Basilica (Ruins)

Harbour

Fort

Fort (Ruins)

Municipal
Baths

Shepherd of Pafos watering his flock a century ago (engraving)

continue its glorious course and develop into today's city.

The only elements concerning the Venetian period is that the Pafos fort was not only abandoned, but was also destroyed so that it would not fall to Turkish hands. Besides, there came a time when invasion and subsequent conquest of the entire island by the Ottoman Turks was a certainty for the Venetians.

During the Ottoman occupancy of the island, Pafos, as well as the whole of Cyprus, fell into decline and many foreign visitors describe it as "a deserted city". The period was characterised by heavy taxation, under development, persecutions, bad administration and, mainly, total indifference on the part of the conqueror. However, during this period Pafos was the seat of a district judge (Kadis) and of an Ottoman pasha (Kaimakamis) while, following the ouster of the Latin Church and the re-activation of the Orthodox Church, Pafos once again became the seat of the Pafos bishop. Furthermore, it is mentioned that, in 1821, a failed revolutionary attempt occurred in Pafos. It is during the Ottoman period that the fort was rebuilt, while other representative for the period features, such as inns, baths and minarets appeared on the Pafos landscape.

The English succession from the Ottomans took place without any incidents or bloodshed. During the Colonial period, which began in 1878, Pafos was recognised as the capital of one of six districts. A Town Hall was established, and the police station, the office of the district commissioner, the hospital, the Lands and Surveys office, the post office, the bishop and other buildings were set up. Piped water made its appearance in the city, newspapers started their circulation, education improved and a number of cultural societies were established. A burning issue was the link-up of Pafos to the road system connecting the other cities and villages of Cyprus. Despite its link-up to Limassol and Nicosia through two coastal roads, the width of these carriageways was inadequate, something which was put right following the establishment of the Cyprus Republic. Even though, during the Colonial period Pafos was one of the main cities of Cyprus, it lacked in facilities and services. It was never able to keep its populace, which abandoned the city in search of other, newer and more profitable opportunities in other cities, primarily Limassol and Nicosia.

In the years following Independence and up to the Turkish Invasion, Pafos continued to be a relatively small city, offering limited services and featuring a limited number of tourists and visitors. However, after 1974, Pafos enjoyed an unprecedented tourist activity following the construction of numerous hotels. Tourist-related industries (restaurants, souvenir shops, night clubs etc.) also enjoyed significant upswing. Upon the completion of the Pafos Irrigation Scheme, the irrigation of a sizeable coastal area surrounding Pafos was made possible, contributing to the agricultural development of the hinterland. Both industry and handicraft, albeit of limited economic potential, contributed to the sudden economic development of Pafos. The 1974 Turkish invasion forced the Turkish-Cypriot residents of Pafos to abandon the city, while at the same time displaced persons from the occupied areas of Cyprus settled in Pafos. It is estimated that approximately 2.000 Turkish-Cypriots left the city, while over 3.000 displaced persons settled there. The sudden increase in the city's population is largely due to the post-1974 demographic changes, to the movement of rural Pafians to the urban centre, and to the development projects of the last two decades.

In this way, while the population of Pafos (both Ktima and Kato Pafos) in 1881 came to 2.204 souls, in 1901 it rose to 3.134 and to 4.467 in 1931. In 1960 it rose to 5.803 and reached 6.989 souls in 1973. The population rose significantly by 1983, reaching 13.112 souls. Based on the most recent census (2001), the municipality of Pafos on its own has a population of 26.530, while that of the wider urban area comes to 47.198 inh.

❏ PAFOS AS A SERVICE CENTRE

As a population centre, Pafos presents an interesting picture. The population figures of the 2001 census, as has already been mentioned, give a total municipality population of 26.530 persons, while the population of the wider urban area amounts to 47.198 persons. The municipality population constitutes about 40% of the total population of Pafos, while the wider urban area constitutes about 60%.

Pafos, the fourth largest town of Cyprus, after Nicosia, Limassol and Larnaka, constitutes about 5,4% of the total population of Cyprus or 8% of the total urban population of the free part of the island. Such a relatively sizeable population undoubtedly exercises influence upon the regional functions of the city as well as on the life and activities of its hinterland.

As an administrative centre, Pafos is the seat of the District Officer and practically all regional offices of the Government, as well as the seat of regional offices of some semi-governmental organisations, a large number of insurance companies, banks etc.

Due to its industrial estate at Mesogi and its industrial zone at Anatoliko, Pafos is a mini-industrial centre.

The presence of all banks of the island in Pafos, the multitude of all kinds of shops and a few supermarkets, have made Pafos a commercial centre.

Following the Turkish occupation of the two major tourist areas of Famagusta and Kyrenia, Pafos developed into a main tourist centre of the island, leading to the construction of a large number of hotels and tourist apartments. These buildings stretch from Pafos harbour to the east of SODAP winery and north up to and beyond the Coral Bay. The airfield of

Enjoying the sunshine and the seascape of Pafos harbour

Pafos has also contributed to the unprecedented tourist activity.

Furthermore, Pafos is the seat of a Bishopric. The bishop, as pastor for the entire district, deals with all matters pertaining to the church, including the upkeep and restoration of churches and monasteries.

Pafos, currently, boasts a significant number of kindergartens, elementary schools, gymnasiums and lyceums, as well as some private and tertiary educational institutes. Its function as an educational centre attracts pupils and students from the entire district.

Nor does Pafos lag as a cultural and artistic centre, as can be seen through its cultural and artistic activity since the beginning of the century but particularly nowadays.

Currently, Pafos does not lag in athletics and sports.

As a centre of entertainment and recreation Pafos, lying close to numerous sites of interest as well as being a coastal town, attracts a number of visitors, local and foreigners.

The increase in population of the city inevitably turned Pafos into a major consumer centre.

Many public utilities and services have been set up in the town, while the hospital and its private clinics satisfy the medical and pharmaceutical needs of not merely its citizens but those of the entire district.

As an employment centre, Pafos rates fourth in Cyprus. Employment is offered in the fields of tourism , construction, industry and the public services.

■ ARCHAEOLOGICAL SITES AND CULTURAL MONUMENTS

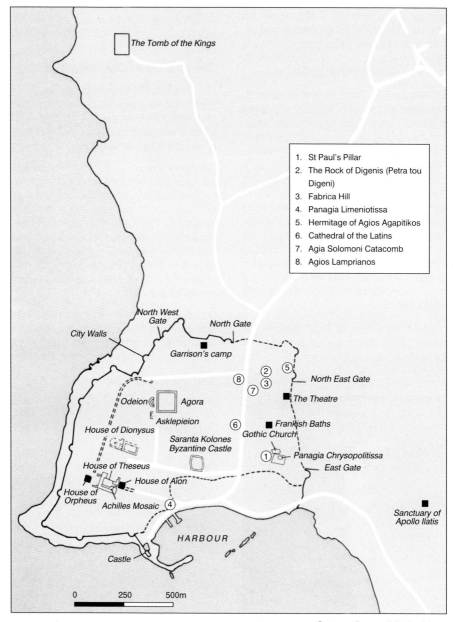

The Tomb of the Kings

1. St Paul's Pillar
2. The Rock of Digenis (Petra tou Digeni)
3. Fabrica Hill
4. Panagia Limeniotissa
5. Hermitage of Agios Agapitikos
6. Cathedral of the Latins
7. Agia Solomoni Catacomb
8. Agios Lamprianos

North West Gate
North Gate
City Walls
Garrison's camp
② ⑤
⑧ ③
North East Gate
⑦
The Theatre
Odeion Agora
Asklepieion ⑥ Frankish Baths
House of Dionysus Gothic Church
Saranta Kolones Byzantine Castle
House of Theseus ① Panagia Chrysopolitissa
House of Aion East Gate
House of Orpheus Achilles Mosaic ④
Sanctuary of Apollo Ilatis

HARBOUR
Castle

0   250   500m

Source: Dept. of Antiquities

31

St Paul's Pillar

West of the church of Agia Kyriaki and whithin the precincts of the large, 4th century Basilica of Chrysopolitissa, stands a column, known as "St Paul's Pillar" where, according to tradition, St Paul was tied and lashed by the Jews.

As known, St Paul together with St Barnabas and Ioannis Marcou journeyed in 45 A.D. from Salamis to Pafos, which was the capital of Cyprus and the seat of the Roman governor of Cyprus, Sergious Paulus. They preached Christianity, as a result of which the Jews turned against them. The blinding of Elymas, adviser of the Governor, as well as the convincing preaching of Paul converted Sergious Paulus to Christianity. A superb painting by Rafael portrays the blinding of Elymas with Barnabas watching the fiery speech of Paul, while Elymas in moments of terror and despondency, lifts his hands to ask for help.

Legend says that St Paul, before the conversion of Sergious Paulus, was given 39 lashes, (saranta para mia) by the Jews. This, however, is not recorded by the Acts. Some speak of only three lashes with a whip having 13 stripes, while others speak of only a lash with a whip which had 39 stripes tied together in three bands.

The basilica of Chrysopolitissa

The basilica of Chrysopolitissa, originally built in the 4th century A.D. with significant modifications until the 7th century A.D., when it was destroyed by the Arab raids, is one of the largest in Cyprus.

Originally the church was seven-aisled, but later was reduced to five-aisles. The original building consisted of a narthex and atrium with porticos and open court around it. The floor of the basilica was covered with colourful mosaics, some of which are preserved. The Arab invasions as well as the subsequent use, during the Middle Ages, destroyed the mosaic floor as well as the walls.

Obviously, such a large basilica had many doors. These entrances together with other details are expected to be revealed by the excavations still going on.

St Paul's Pillar

The Sanctuary of Apollo Ilatis

Basilica of Chrysopolitissa

Most probably the walls of ancient Pafos passed very close to the basilica. Currently, the visitor can observe the columns, the capitals, the mosaics on the floor and the impeccably hewn calcarenite blocks.

The Sanctuary of Apollo Ilatis

The sanctuary of Apollo Ilatis, lying on private property and unknown to most Pafians, constituted a worship place of one of the deities of ancient Greece. Apollo was worshipped in many places of Cyprus, like Kourio, Idalio, Pafos, Tamassos etc, and was regarded as the God of sea, shepherds, medicine, music, song and spiritual life as well as the protector of health and happiness. The God Apollo most probably got the name "Ilatis" from a sacred grove in which his sanctuary was situated.

The sanctuary of Apollo in the eastern necropolis of Pafos consists of two subterranean rockhewn chambers, a rectangular and a circular one, connected with a rock-cut dromos (way). A Cypriot syllabic inscription above the main entrance informs the visitor that the sanctuary was made by the High Priest Tarvas for the God Apollo. The sanctuary dates back to the 4th century B.C., when Pafos was founded.

The Odeion

It lies east of the lighthouse, close to a rocky rise, which might have been the site of an ancient acropolis. Most probably it is the rocky surface that determined the site of the Odeion, which dates back to the 1st century A.D. The Odeion, most probably roofed, was used for musical contests, public orations and plays. It is not certain how many tiers of seats were in the Odeion, though it could accommodate a few thousand. It had most probably been destroyed by the earthquake of the 4th century A.D.

The Asklepieion

The Odeion of Pafos

The Agora

To the east of the Odeion lies the agora or market-place consisting of a colonnaded square courtyard measuring 95x95 metres. The visitor can see the surviving Corinthian columns and capitals, as well as the steps leading to the stoa and the shops. The agora dates to the 2nd c.A.D.

The Asklepieion

The Asklepieion, south of the Odeion, was the healing centre and temple of Asklepios, the mythological God of medicine and healing. It is a building complex with many rooms dating from the 2nd c.A.D.

The Rock of Digenis (Petra tou Digeni)

A strong tradition persists with regard to the solitary rock north of the Fabrica hill, on the way to Pafos harbour, a tradition pertaining to the relationship between Digenis and Rigaina. It is said that Rigaina, whom Digenis desired, had her house built on top of this hill. As in almost all folk tales, Rigaina would only marry Digenis if he managed to transport water for her from some distant location, which in this case was either Mavrokolympos or Tala. Even though this was a Herculean task, Digenis undertook it, transporting the water through clay conduits, traces of which can still be seen east of Chlorakas village. However, Rigaina did not keep her promise, something which enraged Digenis, who threw a huge rock at her from the Moutallos area, which landed right in front of her house. Rigaina riposted with equal rage, throwing her spinning needle, a granite stele, at Digenis, which landed on the fields underneath the Moutallos rise.

The Fabrica Hill

To the left of the main road towards Pafos harbour, there stands a hill featuring large caves and enormous rocks, known as Fabrica.

According to Loizos Philippou, the hill was named as such because, during the Middle Ages, there stood at the site a textile mill, the last remnants of which could still be seen during the last decades of the 19th century.

The underground caves are of sizeable proportions and their coated walls could, at some time, have been painted. Some of the caves are connected, while in others, stair cases bring you to the top of the hill. A number of openings in the roofs of the caves could have acted as skylights. The blackened ceilings and sooty walls could be a later feature.

The Fabrica hill probably dates back, as C. Nikolaou suggests, to Hellenistic

The rock of Digenis

times. It was used during Byzantine times, was quarried in later years and, according to Sakellarios, "its scooped out caves were used as storerooms." Today, however, the hill intrigues every careful traveller, who awaits more research which will shed some light on the uses to which these underground caves were put.

The basilica of Panagia Limeniotissa

The basilica of Panagia Limeniotissa, dating back to the 5th century A.D., lies close to the restaurants of the harbour. The basilica, destroyed by an earthquake in the 12th century, is mentioned by St Neofytos. Currently, the visitor can observe the size of the three-aisled building, the colourful mosaics as well as a few restored columns. The basilica, dedicated to "Virgin Mary of the Harbour", must have been visited by many crusaders and pilgrims on their way to the Holy Land.

The Harbour

The imports and exports of Pafos are no more carried out through Pafos harbour. No more cargo boats visit the harbour, which, currently, is full of colourful fishing boats as well as yachts, mainly from Europe.

In the past, pilgrims arrived in numbers, before proceeding to the temple of Aphrodite at Kouklia. Even Strabo refers to it as the principal port of Western Cyprus. As capital of Cyprus during the Hellenistic-Roman times it must have experienced considerable commercial activity. It was, according to the Ancient Dictionary of Greek and Roman Geography, "a good harbour". In later years it declined and in the Middle Ages it was, as traveller Felix Faber mentions, "abandoned". Sakellarios in the last century described it "as full of sand and stones dropped into it from the old buildings of the town".

The basilica of Panagia Limeniotissa

The harbour of Pafos

Currently, it performs a different task. It is closely associated with present-day tourism, which plays a vital role in the economy of Pafos. Cafés, restaurants and tavernas, around the harbour, cater for a large number of visitors, who come to the harbour for a fresh fish meal, a refreshment or for a stroll along the promenade.

The Garrison's Camp

West of Fabrica Hill, just on the other side of the road, stands the so-called Garrison's Camp. Rock-cut caves similar to those found at the Apollo sanctuary can be seen, believed to date back to the 4th c.B.C. According to one version, the underground rooms belonged to a subterranean altar from the Hellenistic period, while another possible interpretation is that the area was used as a military camp.

Tombs of the Kings

The Tombs of the Kings or the Palaiokastra (Old Castles), as also known, lie to the north-west of ancient Pafos. The site was the necropolis (cemetery) of Pafos with hundreds of underground rock-hewn tombs. Though there is no relation with kings, it is possible that eminent Ptolemies, living in Pafos, might have been buried in the tombs. Crosses and some mural paintings indicate that in early Christian times the tombs acted as refuge of the Christians.

The tombs which date back to the 3rd century B.C., are reached by steps and have open peristyle courts surrounded by burial chambers. As the visitor can observe they are not all uniform. Columns can be either circular or rectangular;

The Tombs of the Kings

some burial chambers are well preserved, while others are utterly destroyed; a stepped road sometimes leads to an arched entrance, while elsewhere it ends up to a carved entrance; the staircase in some tombs is very narrow, while in others it is wide; the recesses or boxes on the cut walls are either small, destined for children, or large for elders.

The Theatre

It lies on the southern slope of Fabrica hill. Recent excavations (1995) have revealed the entire structure, which the visitor can see. Five Greek letters on one of the stone seats indicate that the theatre dates back to the end of the 4th c.B.C. or beginning of the 3rd c.B.C. This proves that the theatre is one of the most ancient buildings of Pafos.

The Frankish Baths

Not far to the south of Fabrica hill, lie the Frankish Baths, dating back to the Lusignan period (1192-1489 A.D.). The baths, which currently retain their original appearance, could accommodate approximately a hundred bathers. It is a well-preserved Frankish building.

Hermitage of Agios Agapitikos

As one explores the Fabrica hill, in its north-eastern corner one observes a cave known as the Cave of Agios Agapitikos.

It is not known if there is any connection between this cave and the sarcophagus in the central square of Pano Arodes village, in the same district, also dedicated to Agios Agapitikos. As in Arodes, also here, next to the cave of

Agios Agapitikos there stood in days gone by the cave of Agios Misitikos and a third one dedicated to Agios Xorinos. The caves of Agios Misitikos and Agios Xorinos, however, were destroyed.

According to tradition, those in love should visit the cave unobserved, leave some coins and take some earth from the cave which they should throw into their desired one's drink. As is the case with Agios Agapitikos in Pano Arodes, for such an escapade to be successful, it should be carried out in complete secrecy, without the help of a third party.

The Cathedral of the Latins (Panagia Galatariotissa)

As one travels from the catacombs to the harbour, the ruins of a Frankish cathedral, possibly of the 14th c., stand on the right hand side. The Latin church is known by the locals as the Madonna of "Galatariotissa" (Virgin Mary of the Milk). The church was restored by Francesco Cantarini, the Latin Bishop of Pafos. Needless to say, during the Frankish and Venetian times, Pafos was the seat of the

The cave of Agios Agapitikos

The Theatre

The Frankish Baths

Relics of the Cathedral of the Latins   *The catacomb of Agia Solomoni*

Latin bishopric and a number of significant church buildings were constructed.

Agia Solomoni catacomb

The catacomb of Agia Solomoni can be found to the left of the Pafos-harbour road, at approximately one kilometre from the medieval fort. Underground chambers were carved out of the limestone, facing onto an open courtyard. These carved chambers resemble those at the Tombs of the Kings.

Loizos Philippou and a number of other scholars refer to graves dating back to the Hellenistic period which were later turned into a catacomb.

The visitor has to descend twenty or so steps to find himself in front of four subterranean chambers, a holy well and an open courtyard. At a later stage the largest chamber was transformed into a church which was, originally, frescoed, traces of which can still be seen today. It is probable that the recesses were also painted with frescoes.

The chamber was transformed into a church during the Byzantine years, and, according to G. Sotiriou, was painted with frescoes during the 9th century. Other authors attribute the frescoes to the 12th century.

A large terebinth tree, several centuries old, grows on the rock above the catacomb. The ailing hang personal articles of clothing, usually handkerchiefs, on its branches, believing that along with these items, they rid themselves of their condition.

City walls

The reproduction of the walls of a city, with a probable history of over 24 centuries, is not an easy task. It is quite possible that the defensive walls of New Pafos were erected during the founding of the city, a date yet unknown, even though it is estimated that Nikokles built the city during the 4th century B.C. The walls of Nea Pafos were probably destroyed in the 7th century A.D., during the Arab raids.

Today, archaeologists' attempts focus on locating the true position of the walls which, for eleven centuries, girted the city and which, at points, reached a height of seven or more metres. Even through it is still too early to establish every detail of the walls, it seems that they began and ended at the Kato Pafos harbour. They began from the medieval fort, followed a westerly and norht-westerly direction

towards the lighthouse, passed by the Fabrica hill and Agios Agapitikos, proceeded towards the Frankish baths, past Panagia Theoskepasti and the Public Baths, and from there made their way back to the fort.

This extensive fortification, especially near the sea, was made up of monoliths, whereas in the interior it was carved vertically on the existing calcarenite.

Research on the north-western section, near the lighthouse, has revealed a large section of the walls carved out of the natural rock outcrop. The north-western gate, with alcoves to its left and right and connected to a water conduit, which would appear to have been connected at its top to some huge door, as well as the bridge connecting the gate to the coast and the necropolis of the Tombs of the Kings, are some of the noteworthy finds

The ancient city walls

The castle of Pafos

of the archaeological pick. It may be that the conduit, following a downhill path from the bridge to the coast, was connected to a sewage disposal system.

On either side of the north-western gate there were two square towers, the southernmost being entirely carved out of the rock. A number of pieces from its upper part have collapsed. The walls were surrounded by a moat, whose true dimensions have been revealed, whereas another entranceway has been revealed between the tower and the walls, leading from the inside to the moat.

It seems that this second opening, very near the main entrance, served as a passageway for the residents of the city when the enormous gate was closed.

Agios Lamprianos

On the other side of the road and opposite the Apollo hotel lies the catacomb of Agios Lamprianos with a similar structure as the other tombs of the area.

The castle

The Pafos castle, with its imposing rectangular shape and its symmetrical small size dominates the picturesque harbour of Pafos.

According to an inscription above the main entrance, the fort was "built by Ahmed Pasha in 1592 A.D.". What we have, though, is a reconstruction on the ruins of a previously existing Frankish fort, sections of which were incorporated in the new building. There exist testimonies that the Frankish fort was blown up and destroyed by the Venetians during the Ottoman invasion, since they were not able to defend it. According to other historians and writers, the fort dates even further back, to the Byzantine era.

History and the geographical isolation of Pafos required the construction of a fort next to the harbour. It may be that this role was originally served by the fort at Saranta Kolones, a few metres north of the present fort. It is even probable that at some stage, once the old fort was destroyed, the present fort was built as a replacement, at a short distance from the original site.

Besides, the Pafos fort did not serve exclusively as a fortification, since some of its rooms were used as prison cells during the Ottoman period, while the British used the building as a storage area for salt. It was later, in 1935, that the fort was declared an ancient monument.

Today, to the east of the fort and at a short distance from it, the visitor can discern the remains of an old construction which probably formed part of the entire fortification.

The fort is, essentially, two-storied. Skylights and five rooms, seemingly two-storied and linked by a wooden bridge, comprise the first floor. The visitor can easily make out the original position of the wooden bridge. Equally obvious are two openings on the floor, communicating with the underground prison cells, a commonplace feature of medieval years. A flight of steps opposite the main entrance leads to the roof of the fort, where there are three rooms. During the Ottoman period, one served as a mosque, while the other two hosted the garrison.

The Byzantine castle (Saranta Kolones)

Saranta Kolones, the Byzantine fort of Pafos, is situated on a tiny rise, a few metres above sea level. The name Saranta Kolones (Forty Columns) derives from the large number of granite columns strewn across the archaeological site.

Archaeological excavations, begun in 1957, have shed light on many aspects of the edifice, even though the true age of the fort, or the archaeological site itself, is still a matter of dispute. Most probably it is a Byzantine fort, probably built during the third quarter of the 7th century A.D., in order to offer protection to the harbour during the Arab incursions.

Today, the visitor to Saranta Kolones discerns a square fort surrounded by external walls and a moat. It features a central courtyard with towers on each of its four corners. The external wall, of considerable thickness, featured eight towers of various shapes, including a five-sided one. Numerous staircases inside the wall lead to the moat. Entrance was effected through the doorway of a horseshoe-shaped tower on the eastern side.

Large amounts of the masonry would have been used by the residents of Pafos for the reconstruction of the city following the 1222 A.D. earthquake. However, the reconstructed arched domes, as well as several staircases point to the existence of upper stories.

Recent excavations have revealed large numbers of iron arrowheads of a medieval type as well as stone catapult projectiles beyond the western wall of the tower. Furthermore, excavations have revealed a covered sewer in the eastern section of the moat, through which sewage from the fort was channelled to the sea.

The fort at Kato Pafos was one of those surrendered to Richard the Lionheart in 1191 and, according to A. Megaw, was later restored. The fort survived the Frankish period, until its collapse during the 1222 A.D. earthquakes. Recent archaeological excavations reveal the functioning of a sugar mill within the fort.

Saranta Kolones Plan

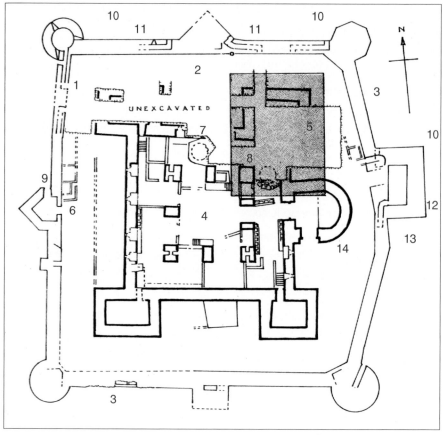

Source: Dept. of Antiquities

1. Entrance
2. Enclosure
3. Curtain walls
4. Main Courtyard
5. Castle
6. Area of Barracks
7. Steam Baths
8. Donkey Mill
9. Postern Gate
10. The Ditch
11. Sally Ports
12. The Gate Tower
13. Site of Bridge
14. Entrance Tower

Mosaics

The house of Dionysus

A visit to the house of Dionysus, lying between the harbour and the lighthouse, is a "must" for every traveller to Pafos. The mosaic decorations and the mythological compositions are the main characteristics of the restored Roman villa, (2nd c.A.D.) unearthed in 1962. The name "House of Dionysus" is mainly due to the many representations of Dionysus, the god of wine. The house most probably belonged to a member of the ruling Roman class or to a wealthy citizen of Pafos. From the architectural point of view it had an open court (atrium) and a cistern (impluvium), a well-planned drainage system and many spacious rooms. The bedrooms, the baths and lavatories were set on the eastern side, while the kitchens and the workshops on the west.

The House of Dionysus was built on the foundations of an earlier Roman house, this being built on the foundations of Hellenistic period. The most important rooms to be seen are:

The Room of Narcissus: This lies in the south-west, to the right as you enter. In the centre of the floor there is an emblem in the form of Narcissus sitting on a rock, close to a spring. According to mythology, Narcissus is wasted away by his unsatisfied love for himself. Gods have changed him into the well-known beautiful flower, known as narcissus.

The Room of Four Seasons: It lies to the right of the Room of Narcissus. Time and space are well represented. The four seasons are represented with busts

Apollo and Daphne. Mosaic of the 3rd c. A.D. (Photo, courtesy of the Dept. of Antiquities)

Ground Plan of the House of Dionysus

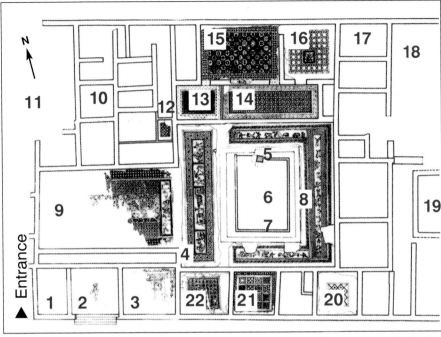

Source: Dept. of Antiquities

1. Scylla Mosaic
2. Narcissus
3. The Four Seasons
4. Pyramos & Thisbe
   Ikarios & Dionysos
   Neptune & Anemone
   Apollo & Daphne
5. Northern Portico
   (Hunting Scenes)
6. Atrium (Open court)
7. Southern Portico
   (Hunting Scenes)
8. Eastern Portico
   (Hunting Scenes)
9. The Triclinium
10. Living Quarters
11. Living Quarters

12. Geometric Scenes
    (black & white)
13. Phaedra & Hippolytos
14. Long Hall (Polychrome
    geometric patterns & other
    motifs)
15. The Tablinum
16. The rape of Ganymedes
17. Private Rooms
    (perhaps bedrooms)
18. Private Rooms
    (perhaps bedrooms)
19. Cistern
20. Mosaics with black & white
    patterns
21. Mosaics with geometric panels
22. Room of the Peacock

linked with water, leaves, flowers or ears of corn, in each corner. Mother Earth is in the middle.

The Room with the Peacock: Further east lies the room of the peacock with open blue-coloured tail.

The Room with the Sixteen Square panels: Here the visitor can admire the decorative compositions.

The Harvest scenes: The visitor returns back to the western section of the House where the Harvest scenes are set. This is a whole world of nature with vines, persons gathering grapes, partridges, hares, animals etc. This room is tied up with the Triumph of Dionysus to the east.

The Triumph of Dionysus: In the centre of the composition is Dionysus, sitting on a chariot drawn by two panthers followed by a Satyr, goat-footed Pan, a naked dark Youth, and two nymphs. The chariot is driven by a Silenus and in front of him an animal tamer, a female figure, a second dark youth and finally a trumpeter.

Between the cistern (impluvium) and the room of The Triumph of Dionysus is a large hall with mythological representations.

Thisbe and Pyramus: This is a scene with vivid colours showing the love of two youths, who in the end committed suicide. Thisbe stands on the left, while Pyramus reclines on a rock with his right hand holding the "horn of Amalthea". His head is crowned with reeds. Between Thisbe and Pyramus is a panther holding in its mouth Thisbes' veil.

Dionysus, Akme and Ikarius: Akme drinks to the health of the seated Dionysus,

Ikarius and "The first who drink wine", 3rd c.A.D. (Photo, courtesy of the Dept. of Antiquites)

ΘΙCΒΗ   ΠΥΡΑΜΟC

Thisbe and Pyramus, 3rd c.A.D. (Photo, courtesy of the Dept. of Antiquities)

while Ikarius pulls a two-wheeled cart loaded with wine skins. Two shepherds got drunk. As the inscription informs us, here were the "first wine drinkers". According to mythology, one day Dionysus visited King Ikarius. On leaving, he donated to him a vine plant and tought him the art of wine-making. When Ikarius produced wine, he decided to test it with others. He wandered to the fields with skins full of wine offering great quantities to farmers and shepherds.

Poseidon and Anymone: Anymone terrified by the Satyr who disturbed her and indicating also her refusal to Poseidon who also fell in love with her, supports her left hand on a rock. The winged cupid attempts an unsuccessful happy compromise.

Peneus, Apollo and Daphne: Daphne is pictured among two deities. The older Peneus appears with a beard, holding in his hand the "horn of Amalthea". Apollo, the god who embodies perfect beauty, chases her.

Hunting scenes: Round the cistern there are scenes of hunting. A scene shows a hunter ready to confront a lion. Two moufflons are being chased by a hunting dog. Movement, energy and vividness distinguish the hunting scenes.

Hippolytus and Phaedra: Here one sees the well-known myth from the homonymous play of Euripides. Phaedra, the stepmother of Hippolytus, fell in love with him. The artist kept both closed to their own world, even though Cupid, to the right of Phaedra, tries to influence further Phaedra's heart.

The hall with geometric decoration: Right of the room of Phaedra and Hippolytus there is a room with beautiful geometric decorations. The artist plays with colours, shapes and combinations creating an astonishingly beautiful composition that attracts every visitor's eye.

The room with geometric shapes: This is another room with geometric shapes where bright colours and vividness of the mosaic compositions predominate. The visitor can discern crosses, shields, circles as well as the "Greek Keys".

Ganymede and the Eagle: Adjacent is the rape of Ganymede by Zeus. Zeus, the father of gods, disguised as an eagle, carries Ganymede to Olympus, the abode of Gods, to serve as wine-bearer to the gods. Ganymede was supposed to be the "most handsome of mortal Men".

Most probably the House of Dionysus was destroyed by the earthquake of the 4th century A.D. Since then the mosaics remained covered until they were restored recently.

(For those who would like to have more details concerning the House of Dionysus, we strongly recommend the book of G.S. Eliades, entitled "The House of Dionysus".)

The House of Theseus

The mosaics of the villa of Theseus lie close to the House of Dionysus and date back to the 2nd century A.D. Apart from the very interesting geometrical decorations, two mosaics depicting mythological representations are worth seeing:

Theseus killing the Minotaur: This mosaic successfully renders the well-known myth

Apollo and Marsyas, 4th c.A.D. (Photo, courtesy of the Dept. of Antiquities)

Ground Plan of the Villa of Theseus

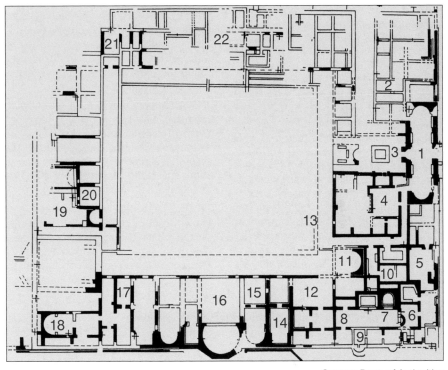

Source: Dept. of Antiquities

1.	Main Entrance	14-15.	Chambers
2.	Dwelling Area	16.	Achilles Mosaic
3.	Atrium	17.	Chambers for residence & storage
4.	Dwelling Area	18.	Chamber for residence. Mosaic of Neptune & Galatea
5.	Latrine room for 12-14 people	19.	Chambers for residence & storage
6.	Oven	20.	Area where marble statues of gods were found
7.	Luxurius Bath	21-22.	North Wing (for the servants & slaves and was used as a laundry & workshop)
8.	Cold Rooms decorated with geometric mosaic		
9.	Steam Bathroom		
10.	Two large Basins		
11.	The Theseus Mosaic		
12.	Chamber		
13.	Fine Geometric Floor		

of Crete. The labyrinth is personified as a bearded man on the right of Theseus. So is Crete, while Ariadne with agony waits to hear the results. Theseus, in the middle of the mosaic, is ready to hit the minotaur-the cruel half man, half bull-with a club.

Achilles' birth: In the centre of the composition Thetis, tired after giving birth, reclines on her bed. Together with Peleus, seated on the throne, they are watching Ambrosia and Anatrophe who prepare the first bath of Achilles. Ambrosia carries water in a jar while Anatrophe holds Achilles, ready to place him in a bowl. The three fates, Clotho, Lachesis and Atropos come to hail the new-born child. The representation of Achilles' birth is considered by some as the forerunner of Byzantine hagiography. Thetis and Peleus will be substituted by Panagia and Joseph, Achilles by Christ and the three Fates by the Three Magoi.

The House of Aion

The mosaics of the House of Aion date back to the 4th century A.D. and lie close to the mosaics of Dionysus and Theseus. The visitor can see geometrical decorations as well as mythological representations. Five mythological scenes are worth observing:

(i) The bath of Dionysus: Hermes holding Dionysus in his Lap, is ready to hand him over to Tropheus and the Nymphs. Three of the five Nymphs represented in the scene, are preparing the bath. Round Dionysus stand Ambrosia, Nectar and Theogonia.

(ii) Leda and the Swan: This is the well known myth of Leda and the Swan with personification of the river Evrotas (seated river god) and Lacedaemonia town (in Peloponnese). Leda, accompanied by three girls, is ready to take her bath in Evrotas river, while Zeus (in the form of

Ground Plan of the House of Aion

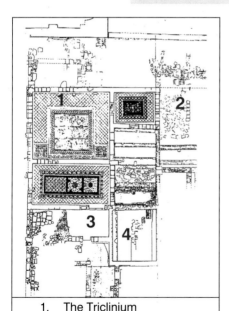

1. The Triclinium.

A.	Presentation of baby Dionysus
B.	Leda & the Swan
C/D.	Beauty contest between Cassiopeia and the Nereids
E.	Musical contest between Apollo & Marsyas
F.	Triumphant procession of Dionysus

1.	The Triclinium
2/3/4.	Chambers for residence

Source: Dept. of Antiquities

Swan) appears to see the naked Leda.

(iii) Beauty contest between Cassiopeia and the Nereids: Cassiopeia boasted that she was prettier than the Nereids. She is finally crowned by Crisis, the personification of Judgement. The Nereids (Doris, Thetis and Galateia), losers of the contest, are carried away by Bythos and Pontos, while a Cupid seated on a bull accompanies them. Aion, in the centre, points to the winner, while Zeus and Athina confirm the victory of the contest.

(iv) Apollo and Marsyas: Marsyas challenged the god Apollo to a musical duel. As known, Apollo was the god of music, and played the lyre remarkably well. As anticipated, Apollo won the duel. In the scene, Apollo, seated on his throne, demands from Scythae to punish Marsyas. Olympos begs for mercy, while Plane stands next to Apollo.

(v) Triumphant procession of Dionysus: The scene shows a chariot led by two centaurs, one of whom plays the lyre while the other holds the pipes. In the same representation appear a maenad, a satyr offering fruit to the God, Tropheus mounted on his mule and a maiden with a basket on her head.

The house of Orpheus

The mosaics of the House of Orpheus belong to the 3rd century A.D. and lie to the west of the House of Theseus. Three mythological scenes are worth seeing:

(i) Orpheus and his Lyre: This is the well-known myth of Orpheus, who, while playing his lyre, charmed trees, birds, and animals. In the scene Orpheus, seated on a rock, plays his lyre, while around him have gathered all sorts of animals, including a lion, a boar, a leopard, a tiger, a deer etc.

(ii) Hercules and the Lion of Nemea: This

Orpheus and the Beasts, 3rd c.A.D. (Photo, courtesy of the Department of Antiquities)

concern the first Labour of Hercules fighting with the lion of Nemea. The hero killed the lion whose hide he always wore.

(iii) The Amazon: The scene depicts an Amazon (daughter of Ares and Aphrodite), with her horse, holding in her hand a double-headed axe.

The house of Four Seasons

The House lies north of the House of Orpheus, and is unfortunately badly damaged. The building was named the "House of the Four Seasons", because the broken mosaic floor represents the personification of the four seasons. The mosaics belong to the first half of the 3rd century A.D. Another mosaic, lying deeper in the soil, represents a hunting scene. A tiger catches in her claws the haunches of an onager, a hunter armed with a spear is ready to face an attacking lion, while a frightened fallow deer runs away from the scene. Another mosaic floor shows, among others, ten animals walking carefree in different directions. The only exception is a dog chasing and biting one of the hind legs of a gigantic hare. A he-goat stands and stares at the spectator in full face.

❑ MUSEUMS

Ethnographic Museum of Pafos

This is a private ethnographic museum, until 1971 known as Folk Art Museum, probably the richest and best private museum in the whole of Cyprus, belonging to Mr George Eliades. Mr Eliades, an intellectual, with interests in archaeology, history, folk art and literature, for over half a century has been collecting art treasures from the countryside of Cyprus, particularly from his native Pafos district, which are currently exhibited in his house, at 1, Exo Vrysi Str, Pafos.

Components of the physical and man-made environment, like natural caves, a Hellenistic rock-cut tomb, a terebinth tree, architecture dating back to 1894 as well as a kiosk, have been incorporated into the ethnographic museum.

The visitor can see costumes, particularly rural costumes and trimmings, traditional carved wooden furniture, farming tools, kitchen utensils, clay artefacts, looms, woven articles, etc. Even archaeological finds, mainly from the Chalcolithic period, are exhibited. For more information, contact tel: 26932010. Open hours: 10:00-17:00 (Monday-Saturday) 10:00-13:00 (Sunday).

Archaeological Museum

The Archaeological Museum of Pafos, housed in a modern building at Leoforos Grivas Digenis, exhibits a vast number of archaeological finds worth visiting.

The exhibits originating mainly from Palaepafos (Kouklia), Nea Pafos (present-day Pafos) and Mario-Arsinoe (Polis) are supplemented by finds from Pegeia, Kisonerga, Lempa, Pano Arodes, Salamiou, Akourdaleia, Pomos, Kidasi, Geroskipou a.s.o.

From the Ethnographic Museum of Pafos

Five chambers are full of interesting exhibits dating from the Neolithic era till the Middle Ages. In the first chamber the visitor examines exhibits from Neolithic, Chalcolithic and Bronze age, including coins cut from the mint of Pafos. In the second chamber are hosted exhibits from the Iron Age and Classical period. A tombstone from Mario with a Cypro-syllabic script, is worth seeing. In the third chamber the visitor can see exhibits from the Hellenistic and Roman periods. Most probably the attention of the visitor could be directed to a marble statue of Asklepios and a marble body of Aphrodite. The fourth chamber hosts exhibits from late Roman and ealry Christian periods, while in the fifth chamber, added recently, there are items from the Byzantine and Middle Ages in general. Tel: 26306215. Open hours: Monday-Friday 08:00-15:00, Saturday 09:00-13:00.

Byzantine Museum

The extremely interesting Byzantine Museum of Pafos lies within the precincts of the Pafos Bishopric. It houses a great number of Byzantine icons, ranging mainly from the 12th to the 19th century, collected from churches and monasteries of the district of Pafos. These icons express the religious faith of the Pafians during the Byzantine era and enlighten present-day visitors on the high artistic quality of those times. The oldest icon, of Virgin Eleousa, from the church of the Monastery of St Savvas tis Karonos, dated about 1200 A.D., is an exquisite example of Byzantine painting.

The Byzantine Museum contains also liturgical books, firmans, manuscripts, wood-carvings, crosses, silver reliquaries, priests' uniforms etc. Tel: 26931393. Open hours: Monday-Friday 09:00-16:00, Saturday 09:00-13:00.

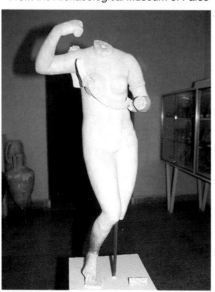

Armoured Aphrodite.
From the Archaeological Museum of Pafos

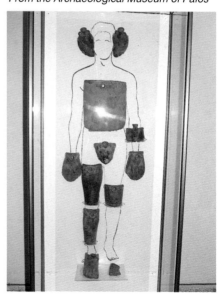

Hot water bottles for each member of the body.
From the Archaeological Museum of Pafos

☐ CHURCHES

Panagia Theoskepasti

It is built on a protruding rock, close to the sea, east of Chrysopolitissa basilica and probably close to the ancient city walls.

As is obvious, lying on such conspicuous rock dominating the scenery, it could be easily discerned by invading Arabs, during their raids. However, according to a legend, the church of God-protected Holy Virgin Mary, was veiled with dark clouds and rendered invisible as soon as the Saracens approached it. When once a Saracen managed to enter the church and tried to steal the golden candle, divine power cut off his hands.

The present-day church of Panagia Theoskepasti was restored on the old foundations in 1928, by preserving its Byzantine architectural style. Though without mural paintings, its wood iconostasis and its precious portable icons continue to attract people, locals and foreigners, who visit the church, particularly to pray to the miraculous silver-covered icon, believed to have been one of the seventy (icons) painted by Evangelist Luke.

Church of Agia Kyriaki

The three-aisled church of Agia Kyriaki, built in the 11th/12th century A.D., lies in the north-eastern corner of Chrysopolitissa basilica. Originally constructed by the Latins, and later transformed into a Greek Orthodox church, particularly after the conquest of Cyprus by the Turks, it acquired a low belfry in 1906.

Panagia Theoskepasti

The western longer side is in striking asymmetry with the Byzantine rhythm of the building, while the dome is unusually higher than that of most classical Byzantine churches. Though not painted, nevertheless some traces of painting indicate that the church might have been entirely covered with paintings.

The interior of the church is simple, though the iconostasis is interesting with icons of St Peter and Paul, Panagia Chrysopolitissa, Our Lord etc. The large icon of Agia Kyriaki lies on the right corner in front of the iconostasis. The church is sometimes known as the church of Crysopolitissa. The church is used by the Anglican Church for regular services by the English-speaking community of Pafos.

MODERN CHURCHES

Agios Theodoros Cathedral

Agios Theodoros Cathedral, close to the Bishopric of Pafos, was built in 1896. In it all the official services take place, particularly on the 28th October, 25th March and 1st April. A war memorial stands outside the church. It has been erected in memory of those slaughtered by the Turks on the 9th July 1821 and those who died in 1912-13 and 1918 wars.

The Bishopric of Pafos

Originally built in 1910 and recently renovated it houses the offices of the Bishopric as well as the Byzantine Museum with its hagiographic treasures. The Bishopric is associated with the resistance movement against the junta during the coup of 15 July 1974. It is from

Church of Agia Kyriaki

the balcony of the Bishopric that Archbishop Makarios and first President of the Republic greeted the crowd after his escape from the Presidential Palace in Nicosia.

Agios Kendeas church

Agios Kendeas church, more spacious than the Cathedral of Agios Theodoros, was built between 1923 and 1930. It lies in Agios Kendeas Str, half-way in Makarios III Ave, on the left hand side, as one travels from Kennedy Square towards the Municipal Market. The saint to whom the church is dedicated is one of the 300 Alaman (German) saints, who arrived in Cyprus from Palestine, in the 12th c., in order to escape persecution by the Saracens. The monastery of Agios Kendeas in Avgorou (Famagusta) is also associated with the saint.

Agios Pavlos church

It is a recently-built church (1970), lying in Pano Pervolia, close to the main road leading to Mesogi. It is Byzantine in style with an impressive dome and many windows on all sides and the dome.

St Anthony's church

In St Anthony Str. lies the church of St Anthony, which is currently used by some Orthodox religious groups for regular services.

The Bishopric of Pafos

Virgin Odigitria, 16th c. From the Bishopric of Pafos

❏ OTHER PLACES OF INTEREST

Municipal Gardens

Many generations of Pafians remember the Municipal Gardens, at the same location, covering approximately the same expanse, opposite the schools, the stele of 28th October and the Municipal Library.

Today, as one walks through the Gardens, one cannot keep up with the great variety of trees and shrubs.

In addition, the traditional fountain, the numerous park benches, the constantly watered grass, the refreshment kiosk and the tennis court also decorate the small area of the Gardens.

The Pafos Municipal Gardens were, early on identified with the celebrations in honour of Costis Palamas, the Greek poet, celebrations which started towards the end of the 1940's. In 1951, Tombros' bust of the poet was erected at the western entrance to the Gardens.

The Town Hall, on the Gardens' northern side, blocks the view of this verdant lung of the city. On the Gardens' eastern side one can see the bust of the first mayor, poet and reformer of Pafos, Chr. Galatopoulos, and the bust of hero, Evagoras Pallikarides, executed in the Central Prisons for his participation in the struggle of Liberation (1955-59).

A Very Impressive Sector of Pafos Town

Between the headquarters of Pafos Police and the central offices of the Cyprus Telecommunications Authority (CYTA), on both sides of Grivas Digenis Ave, lies perhaps the most attractive and culturally most significant sector of Pafos town.

Just opposite the Police Station stands the Public Library and in front stands the Column of 28th October, in ionic style, erected to commemorate the resistance of the Greeks to Italian fascism on the 28th October 1940. On the left side of the Grivas Digenis Ave., as one travels to the offices of the Telecommunications Authority, stand the impressive neoclassical buildings of Demetreion Elementary School, founded in 1928, the gate to the Iacoveion Stadium,

Palamas square, Pafos

"Eros" (Cuppid) opposite the Palamas square

Neoclassical buildings housing primary and secondary schools

constructed in the decade of 1920, the Nicolaideion Gymnasium, built in 1928 and the Gymnasium of Ethnarch Makarios III, built in 1960.

On the right side of the avenue lie the Pafos Town Hall, constructed in 1955 and the Public Gardens. Not far away from the Town Hall in the other corner of the Public Gardens lies, as has already been mentioned, the bust of Costis Palamas, the Greek poet, while in the middle of the small Palamas Square there is a copy of the Sleeping Eros, lying in a pool under a domed structure supported by ionic columns.

Within this cultural sector of Pafos one sees the bust of Solomos, the national poet, in the homonymous Solomos square, the statue of hero Evagoras Pallikarides, who was executed in the Central Prisons for his participation in the Struggle of Liberation (1955-59), the bust of Christodoulos Galatopoulos, the energetic mayor of Pafos, etc.

Turkish baths

The Turkish baths, close to the municipal market of Pafos, functioning until the 1950's, have been restored. A few elder Pafians remember the operation of the baths, before private bathrooms were set up in their own private houses. Externally the baths are fully restored, while inside they will be functioning as an Information and Exhibition Centre for Pafos town.

Dasoudi (copse of Pafos)

The copse to the left of the main road from Pafos to Mesogi, has recently been converted into a modern park, with recreational facilities, flower gardens, a small theatre, a space for wider cultural

performances as well as all types of other facilities including traffic. While many tall pine and cypress-trees have remained intact, other trees and shrubs as well as grass have been planted. A cafeteria is also functioning. The official opening of the park took place in 1993.

Sport grounds and stadia of Pafos

Pafos has two significant sport grounds, strongly recommended to interested foreign visitors. The *Pafiako Athletic Centre,* founded in 1982, has a capacity of 8.000 spectators and caters mainly for football and athletics. The *Aphrodite Indoor Sports Hall* was founded in 1991 and has a capacity of 2.000 spectators. It is mainly used for a large variety of sports, particularly basketball, handball, volleyball, rhythmic and olympic gymnastics. Visitors can make use of the above grounds and stadia through proper contacts. *Pafiako Athletic Centre: 26235412, Aphrodite Indoor Sports Hall: 26663063.*

Pafos Aquarium

The Pafos Aquarium is perhaps small in size compared to other Aquariums worldwide but it is very interesting to visit and learn about the mysteries of marine life.

You can admire a spectacular array of colourful fish from the different oceans, seas and rivers and come face to face with sharks and crocodiles. Many types of fish from the Mediterranean sea and exquisite tropical species display themselves in 72 spacious environmentally friendly tanks.

The column of 28th October with the public library at the background

EXPLORING THE COUNTRYSIDE AROUND PAFOS TOWN

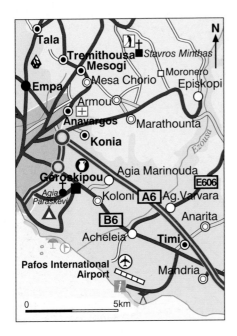

Marathounta. The nucleus of the original settlement is associated with traditional houses, whereas on the periphery modern houses prevail. The view towards Pafos, the proximity to the town and the mild climate have attracted a number of foreign families who have settled in the village.

It is not certain whether the village obtained its name from marathon (fennel) which abounds in the area, though what is known is that hemp was cultivated abundantly in the past.

Hogarth mentions that, at the beginning of the century, he saw a limestone plaque devoted to Apollo Myrtatis (of the myrtle).

Armou, between Mesogi and Marathounta, stands on a rise with an

Entrance to the village of Episkopi

a) Settlements at small distance from Pafos town

> **Route: Konia, Marathounta, Armou, Episkopi, Moro Nero**

Konia is currently expanding close to the built-up area of Pafos with many urban services lying within its administrative boundaries. The houses, built in traditional architecture, are very few. "Anathrika" (Ferula communis) and the special mushrooms associated with it, abound in the area. The view towards Pafos and the sea is vast and panoramic, particularly at night. On a cliff, facing the sea lies the chapel of Five Saints (Agios Avxentios, Evgenios, Evstratios, Mardarios and Orestis).

abundant view towards Pafos. According to Limonidas manuscript, the village is medieval, if we accept the settlement Arino for Armou.

A limestone bowl has been found in Armou on one side of which there is a dolphin's head, most probably belonging to the Roman era. Perhaps the roots of the village date back to the Roman times.

Episkopi, on the west bank of Ezousa river, is a village with a special character. At the village entrance lies a high vertical cliff, appearing as if the rock has been cut with a huge knife.

The settlement was partially ruined by earthquakes in 1953.

Agios Ilarion, one of the notable ancient Christian hermits lived between 290-371 AD, and was a contemporary of Constantine the Great. He spent the last years of his life in Pafos. When Agios Ilarion, who was born in Palestine and travelled to many countries, arrived in Pafos, he first settled in the ruins of the earthquake-struck town and later led the life of a hermit in Episkopi. When he died, at the age of 80, he was buried in his small garden but his student, Isiochos, who lived with the Saint, stole the tabernacle and took it to Palestine. The cave in which he lived can still be seen today and recently a small chapel was built dedicated to Agios Ilarion. Later on a small monastery was built at the foot of the high cliff. It was, however, abandoned and a new church took its place. The village took its name from the diocese created there during Frankish times. As it is recorded, the village was originally called Komi and during the time of King James II (1460-1473) the Orthodox Bishop of Pafos settled there.

Moro Nero is currently deserted. The village was a royal estate during the Frankish times and had an arched church dedicated to Agios Ioannis. The church, with a fallen roof, is next to an earthen road.

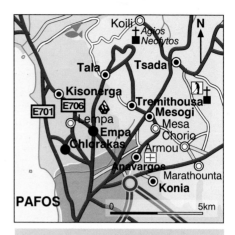

Route: Anavargos, Mesa Chorio, Mesogi, Tremithousa, Tala, Agios Neofytos Monastery

Anavargos, lying north-east of Pafos, is currently part of the municipality of the town. Within the administrative boundaries of the village lies the silo of the Grain Commission, built in 1978 with a height of 27 m and a capacity of 11.000 tonnes. Furthermore, the secondary school of Agios Neofytos and the new hospital of Pafos lie within the boundaries of Anavargos.

Noteworthy is the locality of Pera Vrysi with its huge outcropping rocks, the varied natural vegetation and the rough topography, where pupils from the secondary schools of Pafos used to go on excursion days. The most significant landform, however, is the locality "Ellinospilloi" (Greek caves), south of the village, now fenced and protected. They constituted a necropolis during the Hellenistic-Roman times. They are carved tombs which can be compared favourably with the well-known Tombs of the Kings, in Pafos. Later on some of the tombs were used for worship purposes.

Mesa Chorio, east of Mesogi, is continuously being urbanized with the agricultural land being converted to built-up area. Two churches, the parish church

Basket-weaving, Mesogi

Tala lies south-west of the monastery of Agios Neofytos, the area of which administratively belongs to Tala. Large abandoned areas are being converted into tourist villas and country houses for locals and foreigners alike. *Kamares Village,* for instance, includes about 500 villas, built in traditional architecture, with all services and facilities, including swimming pools, gardens, squares, arches made of hewn limestone blocks, verandahs, tiled roofs and whitewashed walls. It is estimated that the foreign population in Tala is four times that of the locals.

The domed church of Agia Aikaterini, built in the 15th century in a Byzantine style, has a narthex, added later. It was originally covered with frescoes, though today they have disappeared. Agia Aikaterini church is the principal cultural site in Tala.

Agios Neofytos Monastery. St Neofytos was born in 1134 at the village of Kato Drys, near Lefkara. Since the age of 17, he lived in the monastery of Agios Chrysostomos, on the Kyrenia range, as a lay brother cultivating the vineyards.

He believed in ascetic life and soon left the monastery travelling to the Holy Land where, for six months, sought a suitable site of solitude. He returned to Cyprus, back to the monastery of Agios Chrysostomos, which again he left, walking to Pafos with the intention to go, by boat, to Asia Minor and particularly to the mountain of Latros in Ionia. Wandering in the coastal plain of Pafos, he came across a rocky surface with a cave in the present locality of the monastery. The topography, the solitude and the presence of a spring, were considered ideal for his future ascetic life. In a few years time, at the age of 25, he carved his Encleistra (cave) and made it habitable. The cave currently preserves a narthex, the main body of the church, the sanctum and the cell of St Neofytos. In his cell are still preserved his rock-table,

in the centre of the settlement and an older one close to the cemetery, are devoted to Agia Marina. According to tradition, Agia Marina is miraculous in cases of disputes among married couples.

Mesogi, now urbanized, constitutes a suburb of Pafos town. Within the administrative boundaries of Mesogi lies the industrial estate. Within the settlement there have grown restaurants, tavernas, supermarkets, special and general shops, video clubs and a number of other services.

Basket-making, an almost exclusive handicraft of the village, is currently dwindling with a few old women still pursuing this traditional folk art.

Tremithousa is currently joined to the neighbouring Mesogi.

Terebinth, from which obviously the village obtained its name, grows in the village together with carob, almond trees, cereal and some vegetables. It is from the terebinth tree that in the past the well known Pafos chewing gum was produced.

Fresco, Agios Neofytos

the rock platform on which he slept, his library and his burial grave. The paintings of the Encleistra were undertaken by Theodoros Apsevdis. At the age of 65 he carved the "Upper Encleistra", above the main cave where he could withdraw and get rid of the ever-increasing visits. He died at the age of 85.

About 200 years later the main church of the present monastery was built. It is in the 15th century church that the saint's relics are currently preserved. Though the church is devoted to Theotokos Maria, it is known as the church of Agios Neofytos. The church is three-aisled with columns and arches separating the aisles. The iconostasis is of exceptional art.

However, the visitor to Agios Neofytos monastery is probably more interested in the Encleistra. The paintings on the narthex of the Encleistra compel the visitor to stop and study them carefully.

Among them are: The Last Supper, Christ Washing his Disciples' Feet, Abraham Entertaining the Angels, The Betrayal, the Crucifixion, the Resurrection and others.

In the bema one notices, among others, the Pantocrator, various Saints, the Ascension and St Neofytos between the Archangels. The tiny cell of the Saint attracts the attention of visitors. St Neofytos is known as a leading ecclesiastical writer of the 12th century. A letter entitled "Concerning the Misfortunes of Cyprus", is of exceptional historical value, as he describes the occupation of Cyprus by Richard Coeur de Lion.

The close proximity of Agios Neofytos monastery to Pafos and the unique frescoed encleistra (cave) on the vertical rocky cliff, are factors that attract many visitors, particularly foreigners, to the monastery.

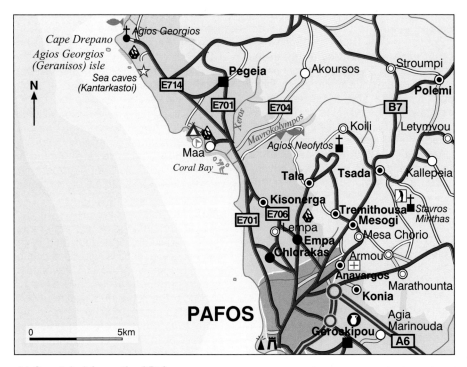

b) Coastal plain north of Pafos

> **Route: Chlorakas, Empa, Lempa,**
> **Kisonerga, Potima, Coral Bay,**
> **Pegeia, Sea caves (Kantarkastoi),**
> **Agios Georgios**

About 3 km north of Pafos lies **Chlorakas,** a large coastal village loaded with history, thrill and memories. As farmers till their land, very often unearth stone implements, axes and pottery which testify a possible Neolithic settlement, not yet disclosed. The remains of Rigaina's aqueduct, between the settlement and the sea, most probably constitutes the last remains of a long aqueduct carrying water from the Mavrokolympos river to Pafos. Close to the village square, next to the modern church of Panagia Chryseleousa, stands the old medieval church of Panagia. Above the west door there is a coat of arms. The dome, the cruciform shape, the

worn out frescoes and the gilted iconostasis continue to fascinate the visitor.

At the entrance to the village, as one comes from Pafos, stands the tiny, whitewashed, Byzantine church of Agios Nikolaos with some traces of frescoes. It can hardly accommodate ten persons in it.

Chlorakas is associated with the Struggle of Liberation (1955-59). It is on the coast of Chlorakas that Grivas, the EOKA military leader, landed in 1954, while at the same place the boat Agios Georgios, carrying ammunitions, arrived a few months later. The boat is currently kept under a shelter, while nearby lies a newly-constructed church devoted to Agios Georgios. Currently, west of the village, on a conspicuous location, modern villas, belonging mainly to foreigners, have been built, while by the coastline new hotels have appeared.

Empa, 4 km north of Pafos, was, according to Mas Latrie, a village where sugar-cane was cultivated during the Frankish times. It was also the seat of one of the five sub-districts into which Pafos was divided. The most important monument of the village is the Byzantine church of Panagia Chryseleousa, three-aisled with two domes. Its belfry is recent and relatively low, while an external staircase-something unusual for a church-leads to the roof. The interior of this stone-built church is rich in treasures and mural paintings. A holy Gospel, leather-bound, issued in Venice in 1539, is preserved in the sanctum.

Unfortunately, the original paintings of the 12th century are not preserved. Present-day paintings as well as portable icons belong to the 15th and 16th centuries. The visitor can observe, however, the successive strata of mural paintings. The 17th century iconostasis contains some icons dated 1736 A.D. with an earlier one belonging to Saint Symeon Stylites.

A noteworthy icon is that of Christ holding a Gospel in his left hand. Some specialists consider this icon as one of the most beautiful icons of Cyprus. The icon of Panagia (Madonna), John Theologos and John Prodromos are very fascinating too. A fine icon painted on two panels with the Apostles, six on each panel, hangs in a glass case.

The paintings are very interesting with the impressive Christ Pantocrator on the dome surrounded by Angels. A fresco representing the miracle of fishing is worth noting. In the boat, there are six apostles carrying a net full of fish, while before Christ kneels Peter.

About 150 metres east of the village, following a narrow track, the visitor can reach a vaulted chapel dedicated to St George. Traces of paintings, belonging to the 16th century, prove that the chapel was originally entirely covered with paintings. The sanctum is square, round a holy stone altar. Three recesses in the north, south and east wall were most probably used as tombs. The chapel lies close to a rocky surface, surrounded by asphodels, cyclamens and giant fennels.

Lempa, about 5 km north of Pafos, is a beautiful small village with some peculiarities. The village is well-known in

Panagia Chryseleousa, Byzantine church, Empa

Kisonerga banana plants

the art circles because here artist Stass Paraskos founded the Cyprus College of Art, accepting and training art students from all over the world.

Lempa is also widely known because of its Chalcolithic settlement of 3500-2500 B.C. at the locality "Lakkous". The visitor will be able to observe the circular buildings which were supported by posts. They were inhabited by a farming community which cultivated wheat, barley, olives, grapes and legumes. It is remarkable that the prehistoric people of Lempa had overseas contacts and they had developed artistic and religious traditions. They buried their dead underneath the floor or just outside. The environment of Lempa provided everything the inhabitants needed for their everyday life. They used stone axes for the clearing of forests, adzes for carpentry and mortars and querns for grinding cereals, lentils etc. Archaeological excavations are still going on in the village. The visitor will be able to see on spot a restored village of the Chalcolithic period with all details concerning the construction of houses and the material used.

Lempa was, according to Mas Latrie, a royal estate during the Frankish period with sugar-cane cultivated in the irrigable parts of its administrative land.

Kisonerga, rich in physical and cultural features, was, according to Mas Latrie, a royal estate during the Frankish period. On a rise, close to the sea, at the locality Vikla, there was a Byzantine tower, which was functioning as an observatory. Its traces, however, have vanished.

Close to the church of Transfiguration lie the ruins of a tiny chapel dedicated to Zinovia and Filonilli. These two saints, close relatives of St Paul, accompanied him from Tarsus to Pafos and worked with him for the spreading of Christianity. They died and were buried at Kisonerga while St Paul was at Pafos. The holy well, mentioned by Tsiknopoullos and Gunnis, cannot be traced close to the single-aisled chapel.

The deep roots of the village lie at the locality Mosfilia where a prehistoric settlement has been unearthed dating back to the fourth millenium B.C. (from the end of the Neolithic to the beginning of the Chalcolithic period).

Circular houses with a very large diameter have been unearthed. The roofing of such huge buildings no doubt presupposes special architectural knowledge. A cobbled road discovered supplies insights into public enterprise and communal organisation in Cyprus about 3000 B.C. Moreover excavations at another locality "Myloudkia" yielded painted stonework and other evidence of the early Chalcolithic period. Kisonerga is the first village in Cyprus to implement land consolidation, a revolutionary project that helped farmers to group up their scattered plots of land, thus, creating compact holdings served by a new road network.

Many remunerative crops are grown in Kisonerga including bananas, vegetables and citrus.

A few hotels appeared recently transforming Kisonerga into a tourist village.

Potima, a huge estate in Frankish time, was converted to a chiftlick during the Turkish period. It was expropriated by the British Government in 1945 and later redistributed and rented to landless or small holders from Kisonerga and Pegeia. It is currently being cultivated with bananas, citrus and vegetables.

In the south-eastern corner of the chiftlick, known as *"Kleidotoudes",* there are fossils of pigmy hippopotamus (Hippopotamus minutus), which lived in Cyprus until recent geological times. The animals lived close to a shallow lagoon, that existed during the Pleistocene era. Most probably abrupt climatic changes brought about the extermination of the animals. Currently, if you dig a few centimeters in the soil, you will find fossils of this pigmy hippopotamus.

Coral Bay is a horse-shoe cove with its two edges ending in abrupt cliffs, while in the middle an extensive fine-grained sandy beach is bordered by the rock of coral limestone. This explains the name of the bay and the beach. From the two edges of the cove, the view is extensive and panoramic.

Coral Bay

Sea caves (Pegeia)

On the northern edge of the cove, which is a tiny peninsula with cliffs on three sides, the ancient settlement of Maa-Palaiokastro has been unearthed, which dates back to the 13th century B.C. Achaean settlers, after the decline of Mycenean centres in Peloponnisos (Morea), arrived in Cyprus, mainly attracted by its copper mines. The archaeological excavations unearthed a large architectural complex comprising large as well as small rooms communicating by a common corridor. They chose this strategic position to build their fortified settlement, which was however, soon abandoned, most probably in the first decades of 1200 B.C.

The museum of Mycenean Settlement has recently been set up in the area exhibiting Mycenean finds and various charts indicating internal and external trade during that period. It is worth visiting the museum.

Pegeia, about 5 km north-east of Coral Bay, has grown around a spring, the much-sung "Spring of Pegeia Women". The spring preserves its arches and a stone-built tank where adequate quantities of water could be stored.

About 3 km west of Pegeia there was in the past the monastery of the All-holy Virgin Mary Zalagiotissa. Currently, only the place-name is retained. North-west of the Coral Bay, within the administrative area of Pegeia, lies

Wild vegetation (Pegeia)

chalky rocks encouraged the waves to open caves which now constitute labyrinthine formations, with some of them communicating inside. Until sixty years ago, as the locals say, there were a few seals living in the caves. There is an earthern road left of a new tiny settlement (with the same name) on the Pafos-Agios Georgios road which takes you to the caves. Pegeia is, currently, being developed not only agriculturally (produces bananas, table grapes, citrus and vegetables) but touristicaly as well.

On the way to Agios Georgios isle, close to BP petrol station, lies the recently established Reptile Park (Snake George's Reptile Park) where visitors can observe cypriot reptiles, particularly snakes.

Agios Georgios (Pegeia)

About 8 km north-west of Pegeia, the traveller will encounter a tiny settlement with cafés, restaurants, a few isolated households, a guest house and a modern, whitewashed church dedicated to St George. The church is much venerated by the people of the surrounding villages.

Besides, there is a fishing-shelter with a few colourful fishing boats. The tiny beach close by caters for the swimmers who arrive there in hundreds during the summer months. Just opposite, in the sea, lies he picturesque isle, of Geronisos or isle of St George, at a distance of about 300 metres. The surface of the tiny isle has the same height as the surface of the mainland, a fact that explains how it was formed and how strong the power of the stormy waves is. The fauna of the isle consists of sea-gulls, rock doves and a few serpents, while the surface is covered with lentisk, thyme and various herbs. Besides, on the isle there are wells, cisterns and foundations of houses, most probably of an ancient public building. Most of the findings, so far, belong to the Hellenistic period, though it is strongly believed that at the end finds from the

---

AVAILABLE IN PEGEIA (including Coral Bay)

Bank
Camping site (Feggari)
Co-operative Credit Society
Hotel/Tourist Apts
Municipality
Petrol station
Pharmacy
Restaurant
Stadium

Keratidi, a tiny shelter from where, until recently, large quantities of carobs were exported. Presently, only the ruined store-houses are preserved. About 2 km north of Pegeia, on the way to Kathikas and the Laona plateau, lies the small forest of Pegeia covered with juniper and pine-trees. The view from this point towards the sea is almost unique. About 2 km south of Agios Georgios church (Cape Drepano) lie the most spectacular sea caves of Cyprus, known as **Kantarkastoi caves of sea caves of Pegeia**.

Cracks and joints in the strata of the

Chalcolithic period will be unearthed as well. Archaeological excavations are still going on.

A series of early Christian rock-cut tombs below the cliff, close to the church, with rectangular or vaulted openings, belong, most probably, to early Christians or hermits. For the cultural point of view the most impressive site in the area are the three basilicas of the 6th century A.D. close to the church of Agios Georgios. The middle one, of large dimensions, preserves beautiful mosaics with animal, bird and fish representations as well as other geometric shapes. The baptistery, the columns, the underground reservoir where rain water gathered, the bath complex with cold and warm water as well as the mosaics, are the findings of the latest excavations. From the excavations, still in operation, it is, so far, concluded that the settlement was at its growth during the late Roman-early Christian period, but did not survive the Arab raids of the 7th c.A.D. Though the area is fenced, the visitor can observe the basilicas and can contemplate on the possible dense population living in the area with such a spacious basilica.

Agios Georgios offers accommodation, a few restaurants specialising in fish meals, cafés and snack bars.

St George isle (Pegeia)

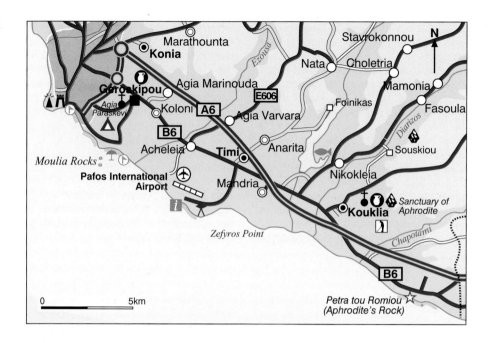

c) Coastal plain south-east of Pafos

> **Route: Geroskipou, Agia Marinouda, Koloni, Acheleia, Agia Varvara, Timi, Pafos International Airport, Mandria, Achni, Petra tou Romiou**

Geroskipou according to tradition, implied even by the name of the village, was the site where the holy gardens of the Goddess Aphrodite lay. Pilgrims from Nea Pafos passed through Geroskipou before reaching the temple of Aphrodite, at Kouklia (Palaepafos). At Geroskipou, in the holy gardens of the Goddess, donations, sacrifices and many other activities in honour of Aphrodite were taking place. Even currently a cave in the village is called "Bath of Aphrodite".

Strabo mentions Geroskipou, calling the settlement "Ierokipis". Many other travellers have written that in the coastal plain of Geroskipou, until the last century, there were centuries-old olive and carob trees.

In the 11th century A.D. the five-domed Byzantine church of Agia Paraskevi was built, somewhere in the middle of present-day settlement.

It is also mentioned that at Moullia, a coastal locality of Geroskipou, the miraculous icon of Panagia Chrysorrogiatissa was found by the monk Ignatios, who carried it to Rogia mountain from where the monastery took its name.

In 1800 Sir Sydney Smith visited Geroskipou and was so much impressed by the resident Zimboulaki, that he appointed him as vice-consul of Britain. Zimbulaki, who was born in Kefalonia, settled in Geroskipou and his duties as vice-consul were to protect the interests of Britain. The house of Zimboulaki where many personalities were hosted, was bought in 1947 by the Department of Antiquities to be converted into Folk Art Museum.

In 1925 a British firm set up a factory for silk production. Hundreds of workers both from Geroskipou and the surrounding villages were employed in it. However, the factory closed in 1952. It is also mentioned that at Geroskipou there was also a linen-processing factory.

The village is the centre of the famous tasty Geroskipou turkish delights, displayed on stalls on both sides of the road. The industry was established in the previous century.

The industry commenced in 1895 by a single family, while currently a few families, descendants of the original family, manufacture turkish delights. It is said that there is a secret in the making of the very tasty and unique Geroskipou turkish delights, passed on from generation to generation.

Turkish delights, Geroskipou

Kato Brysi, the original fountain of the village, before piped water was introduced to all houses, is an architectural and historical monument.

Present-day Geroskipou is changing rapidly. A large area of the village is irrigated by the Asprokremmos dam, which encouraged new remunerative crops, like table grapes, citrus, bananas and vegetables. Tourism is expanding rapidly, particularly along the sea coast.

The **Church of Agia Paraskevi.** Special mention of the five-domed principal church, of Agia Paraskevi, at the centre of the village, is necessary. The church, built in cruciform style, dates back to the 11th century. The stone-built, low belfry dates back to 1886. According to L. Philippou, the west end of the church was extended in the 19th century and enlarged in 1931. A structure erected to the right of the altar and attached to the main church was formerly used as a baptistery. Most probably the edifice of Agia Paraskevi was built on the foundations of an ancient temple, as hinted by G.S. Frankoudis and Sakellarios. The best preserved paintings are: The Nativity of Christ, the Baptism, the Crucifixion, the Resurrection of Lazaros, The Last Supper, Judas

Betraying Christ, Christ before Pilate a.s.o. There is also a noticeable portable icon, probably of the 15th century, which on one side portrays the All-holy Virgin Mary with the Child and on the other side the Crucifixion with unusual colours.

The **Folk Art Museum** is housed in a traditional Cypriot house which originally belonged to Cephalonian Andreas Zimboulaki, a resident of the village, appointed vice-consul by commander Sir Sydney Smith. Half of the house was purchased, as mentioned, by the Department of Antiquities in 1947 while the other half was acquired after 1974. It commenced functioning as a Folk Art Museum in 1978. All rooms are full of displays of the Cypriot civilization, particularly of the last two centuries. The Museum hosts costumes, agricultural tools, house utensils, wood carvings and so on.

Agia Marinouda, six km south-east of Pafos and east of Geroskipou is currently undergoing tourist and agricultural development.

Koloni, irrigated by the Asprokremmos dam, specialises on table-grapes, potatoes, citrus, flowers, peanuts and vegetables.

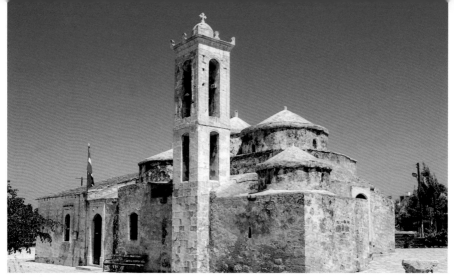

Five-domed church of Agia Paraskevi

Within the administrative boundaries of Koloni lie Anatoliko, an annex of Agios Neofytos Monastery, the slaughter-house of Pafos and two potteries, functioning on a commercial basis.

The potteries are located on both sides of the main settlement road. Travellers can stop and buy souvenirs, if they like.

GEROSKIPOU ZENON GARDENS CAMPING

It is situated about 3 km east of Pafos, on the beach, next to Geroskipou Tourist Beach. It has a capacity of 95 caravans or tents and currently functions between April and October. Entrance to the camping is €10 per couple. It is equipped with car parking, toilets, shower and washing facilities, piped drinking water, mini market, cafeteria/restaurant.

Acheleia is known for its large estate or its chiftlick of about 640 hectares, lying between Geroskipou and Timi, irrigated by Ezousa river.

Though the land tenure of this chiftlick is not known particularly during the Byzantine period, nevertheless, during the Frankish era it was either a feud or a royal estate. It belonged also to the Grand Commandery. During the Frankish-Venetian period the extensive fertile land of Acheleia was cultivated with sugarcane. The production of sugar was destined for Venice and was particularly handled by the commercial firm of Martini, in Venice.

During the Turkish times Acheleia was a chiftlick expropriated by the British in 1945. After the independence of Cyprus, the land was divided into compact holdings and distributed to farmers.

Within the administrative area of the chiftlick or close by stand three churches: that of Agios Georgios, built in 1743, close to the main Pafos-Limassol road, the chapel of Agios Theodosios, of cruciform style, stone-built with a number of worn-out frescoes on its walls, and the ruined chapel of Agios Leontios near the coast. On the right bank of Ezousa river, stands **Agia Varvara,** an originally mixed village. An open canal, parallel to the river bed, constituting part of the Major Pafos Irrigation Project, has recently been constructed.

A large area of **Timi** is irrigated by the Asprokremmos dam with a huge water-tower and a canal vividly stamped on its landscape. The beach of Timi attracts a number of bathers from Pafos as well as other tourist areas. Close by is the picnic site of Timi with adequate facilities. The forest of Timi, composed of eucalyptus and acacias lies next to the beach.

The original church of Agia Sofia, close to the centre of the settlement and not far away from the modern church of Agia Eirini, was originally covered with mural paintings, before being converted to a mosque by the Turks in 1571.

TIMI PICNIC SITE

It is situated one km on the right hand side of the road of Pafos International Airport to Timi (on the beach by an eucalyptus tree forest). It has a capacity of about 600 persons. It is equipped with car parking, toilets, piped drinking water, tables and benches, barbecue facilities and children's play areas.

The **International Airport of Pafos** has been constructed on land belonging to Timi and Acheleia settlements, after a Government decision in 1979. It lies on flat land, close to the sea with abundant visibility. The decision was taken particularly after the development of tourism in Pafos-Polis and the agricultural development of Pafos coastal plain with the implementation of irrigation and other infrastructural works.

The functioning of the airport began in 1983 and serves two main purposes: It serves tourist movement particularly to and from european countries as well as the export of fruit and vegetables mainly to Britain, Scandinavia as well as other European countries. It can host all types of aircrafts within its 2.700 m corridor which has a width of 45 m. The store facilities are adequate and all other amenities are abundant.

PAFOS INTERNATIONAL AIRPORT

The Airport is 13 km east of Pafos town, 56 km from Limassol, 122 km from Larnaka, 45 km from Polis and 137 from Nicosia. The main services offered to travellers are the following:
–Tourist information
–Foreign exchange
–Card and Coin-operated telephones
–Duty free shops
–Cafeteria
–Transportation
–Hotel reservations and bookings
–Special facilities for handicapped travellers
–Health Inspector's Office

Mandria. The visitor enters the settlement under the arches of cypress-trees which, together with other cypress and tamerisk-trees, have been planted as wind-breaks.

Around the central village square stand the coffe-shops, the mosque without minaret and the modern church of Agios Andronikos.

Close to the coast lies the modern chapel of Agios Evresis, while the old chapel cannot be traced. Close to the chapel, a rounded hillock and many caves most probably betray the old settlement of Arsenoe. Close by is also the Zefyros point and further west the beach of Timi.

Achni. The cove between Chapotami and Diarizos, south-east of Kouklia, mentioned, though not named, by Strabo, is called Achni.

Most probably pilgrims arriving at Achni joined those from Nea Pafos and together followed the same path towards the temple of Aphrodite during the festival of "Afrodisia". Achni, administratively belongs to Kouklia.

Petra tou Romiou (Rock of Romios), at the extreme south-eastern part of Pafos, close to the district boundaries of Pafos-Limassol, is probably the number one place of interest in Pafos. The rock is loaded with myth, tradition and memories. The whole island is linked with

this rock formation. The fruitful Greek imagination, wise and infallible in its creative conceptions, chose out of all Greek islands Cyprus, as the birth place of the Goddess of Love and Beauty. It is surprising that there is no geological relation of the rock with the adjacent rock formations. This partly explains the tradition that the Rock was thrown there by the Byzantine hero Digenis Akritas. The coastline around is beautiful and

laced and on it break the waves with the foam they create. The waters of the sea, particularly in the summer months, are clear. On these waters are mirrored, late in the evening, the silhouettes of the neighbouring hills under the light of a star-embroidered sky. The gentle slopes are covered with low natural vegetation, particularly of lentisk and thyme. Most probably in the past the slope was covered with thicker and taller natural

Petra tou Romiou

vegetation. It is Eratosthenis who passed the information to us that the whole of Cyprus was covered with forests.

It is from this white foam of the waves that Aphrodite (Venus) was born. She emerged from the foam, and the gold-dressed Horae received her with joy. They placed on her head a beautiful gold crown. Finally she came to rest at Kouklia (Palaepafos) where her temple, currently ruined, is found. The rock is visited every day-summer and winter-by tourists. They come here to look at and admire the coastline where the Goddess Aphrodite was born.

A restaurant close by on the slope, serves visitors. The view from the restaurant is extensive and majestic. Though the waters of the sea near the Rock are deep, nevertheless, sunbathing or swimming in the exact locality Aphrodite was born, is always a challenge and an unforgettable experience.

Route: Kouklia (including its archaeological and cultural monuments)

Kouklia is the settlement that impresses with its large number of monuments. The modern settlement itself stands on the ruins of Old Pafos (Palaepafos) with its temple of Aphrodite. Here lies the famous grand temple of the Goddess of Love and Beauty, which served people for hundreds of years until the advent of Christianity.

Close to the temple of Aphrodite lies the manor house of Frankish period, known as chateau of Covocle. The visitors can focus their attention to the following: *(i) the Temple of Palaepafos, (ii) The Lusignan Manor House, (iii) the Museum, (iv) The church of Katholiki, (v) The Encleistra, (vi) The pierced stones.* The land around was cultivated with sugar cane which was refined in the sugar-mills, unearthed recently west of the Pafos-Limassol main road. As Mas Latrie states, Kouklia was a royal estate during the Lusignan period as well as a geographical and administrative centre for the region. It is in the chambers of the manor house that the Museum of Kouklia is presently housed.

The Temple of Palaepafos. The area around present-day Kouklia, as witnessed by findings unearthed, was inhabited continuously since the 15th century B.C. Though Kouklia is an interesting village, it is nevertheless, the worship of Aphrodite, the dynasty of Kinyrades, and the "Afrodisia" ceremonies which impress and attract visitors to the village. The ruins in their present condition stretch south of the settlement up to the chateau of the Lusignans. The huge hewn blocks of stone, the thick walls, the large courtyards, the capitals and the subsequent mosaics impress, though the original architecture of the temple cannot be surmised. The original arrangements

The Lusignan manor house, Kouklia

Relics from the Sanctuary of Aphrodite, Kouklia

Clay-bath, Kouklia
(From the Arch. Museum of Kouklia

of the temple were, however, quite altered by later Roman changes and additions, when earthquakes necessitated extensive repairs. In fact little remains today of one of the most famous temples of antiquity.

A careful study discloses a large open courtyard with two arcades north and south as well as a few rooms at the north-eastern section. Most probably the huge blocks of stone, particularly those to the eastern edge of the south arcade, belong to the temple that dates back to the beginning of the 12th century. It is in this section that the large sacred cone was found, which, as believed, was the symbol of Goddess Aphrodite. The sacred cone-shaped symbol was always kept veiled and no one was allowed to look at it. It was believed that it was miraculous. The Kinyrad dynasty were the rulers and high priests of the shrine for hundreds of years.

Their power was enormous and lasted up to the Ptolemaic era.

For the links of Cyprus, particularly of Pafos with the Greek World, Homer mentions the breast-plate of exceptional craftsmanship, donated by Kinyras to Agamemnon, the Chief General of the Trojan War. Who, however, was the founder of the shrine of Palaepafos is not clear. A source from Pausanias mentions Agapinor from Arcadia as the founder who arrived at Pafos after the Trojan War. The worship of the Goddess of Love and Beauty was well known to the ancient world. Though there were many ceremonies in honour of Aphrodite, the most important was the "Afrodisia," which attracted people from Cyprus and abroad. The Afrodisia festivities were an annual event and lasted for four days. Pilgrims gathered at Geroskipou and Achni and from there they altogether reached the shrine. From many sources it seems that the festivities consisted of musical, poetic and athletic contests and sacrifices to the Goddess, while the priests issued their oracles. Goddess Aphrodite was associated with life, love and fertility. She remained throughout centuries the par excellence Goddess of the Cypriots.

The Lusignan Manor House

This is a 13th century building, used as the manor house of the Lusignans, who established sugar-cane plantations in the fertile land between the sea and the present-day settlement. Its history is tied up with adventures. In 1426 A.D. it faced the attack of Mamelukes who caused considerable damage to the building. The Turks later on transformed the original edifice, which, as Sakellarios writes, was used as stables for camels and animals. The south sector was recently restored with impressive stone arches in front of a narrow corridor. The remains of the original chateau lie in the eastern section

Leda and the Swan

*Conical stone serving as cult idol
in the Sanctuary of Aphrodite*

From the first floor of the building the visitor can observe the plainland where sugar-cane was cultivated for almost five centuries, up to the 16th century. Almost all the production of sugar from Pafos and Limassol was exported mainly to Venice. Immediately after the 16th century and particularly after the conquest of Cyprus by the Turks in 1571, sugar-cane was superceded by cotton and silk, while later the area was totally abandoned and deserted.

Recent excavations of the Swiss-German Archaeological Expedition unearthed the sugar-cane refinery, west of the present-day settlement, at the locality "Stavros". One of the sugar-mills functioned with the help of animal power while the other by running water. The rooms of the factory, where pots were washed and cleaned, were also unearthed. Thousands of conical pots were unearthed though similar pots were also found close to the temple of Aphrodite. It appears that the initial stage of sugar refining was done close to the mills, while more refined procedure was performed at a different spot close to the temple of Aphrodite.

The Museum. In the chambers of the Museum, the visitor can observe rich samples of ceramic, inscriptions in Cyprosyllabic script on marble as well as on limestone, capitals, swords, mosaics, statuettes, clay lamps, clay idols, Mycenean stone instruments and many other findings from the wider area of Palaepafos.

The church of Katholiki. The church of Katholiki, is a medieval building which served the Latin community. It dates back to the 12th century, though its western section was restored in the 16th century. Currently, the church is long and single-aisled with dome. In essence the visitor sees a cruciform church and an arched sector extending west. Stones from the temple were used for the building of the church, judging from the inscription on

where a large Gothic chamber with long narrow skylights is found. This chateau is regarded as one of the most beautiful remnants of Frankish architecture in Cyprus.

The original square shape of the medieval building is preserved, though changes brought about helped to house the Museum of Kouklia as well as the staff of the archaeological expeditions which still work at Kouklia.

The Temple of Aphrodite

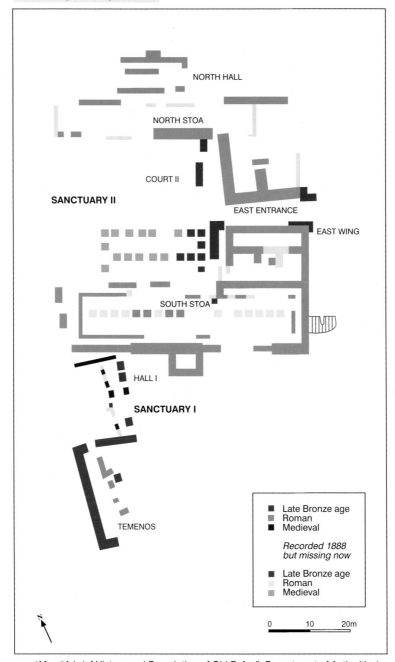

NORTH HALL

NORTH STOA

COURT II

SANCTUARY II

EAST ENTRANCE

EAST WING

SOUTH STOA

HALL I

SANCTUARY I

TEMENOS

Late Bronze age
Roman
Medieval

*Recorded 1888
but missing now*

Late Bronze age
Roman
Medieval

0   10   20m

N

(After "A brief History and Description of Old Pafos", Department of Antiquities)

Pierced stones, part of very old olive press (Kouklia)

some hewn limestone blocks. Most probably none of the original 12th century frescoes are preserved. On the contrary, what the visitor observes are traces of the 16th century paintings. One can discern Pantokrator, on the dome with traces of paintings around, Agios Therapon righ of the iconostasis, the rivers Tigris and Euphrates on the west wall depicted as heads with streams of water issuing from the mouths, traces of Agios Georgios etc. In 1993 the church was restored by the Department of Antiquities.

The Encleistra. About 3,5 km north of the settlement, at the base of a deep valley there is a rock-hewn cave, known as encleistra. It is not certain whether this has been the first choice of St Neofytos before choosing his encleistra at Tala (St Neofytos monastery). A few frescoes are preserved in the cave.

The Pierced Stones. Noteworthy is the monument of the two pierced stones, at the locality Styllarka, in the area of the Kouklia chiftlick. Until recently the stones were considered to be associated with the worship of Aphrodite. They were visited by barren women and girls who had lost their lovers. It has recently been proved that they were olive presses.

The visitor will be able to observe, on spot, the two stones with the reservoirs at their base, where olive oil was collected.

AVAILABLE IN KOUKLIA
Co-operative Credit Society/Bank
Improvement Board
Museum
Police station
Restaurant
Stadium
Petrol Station

EXPLORING THE CHRYSOCHOU AREA

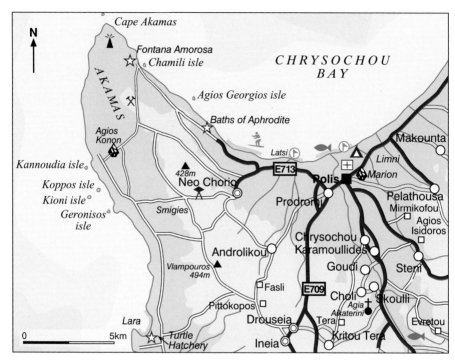

a) Along the Chrysochou valley

Route: Polis, Chrysochou, Karamoullides, Goudi, Choli, Skoulli

Polis. Somewhere in the middle of Chrysochou bay, and between the Pafos forest on the right and the Akamas peninsula on the left, lies a small ancient town which was built thousands of years ago. Today it is called Polis; in the Hellenistic and medieval times it was called Arsinoe and in ancient times it was known as Mario.

Polis, currently sparsely-populated, remained a large farming village for centuries and its trading activities were rather limited, involving non-agricultural dealings with the Limni mine, which has now ceased to operate. Today it is engaged in tourism, offering its mild climate and its almost unlimited sandy and pebbled beaches to the holidaymakers from the cold northern European countries.

The three churches of Apostolos Andreas, Agios Nikolaos and Agia Kyriaki, the modern schools of Higher Education, the new stadium and hospital, next to the general stores and special shops, and the public services, offer the visitor a picture of a small town.

Recently, systematic excavations have started and are continuing. Near the town's hospital, a 6th-century basilica was unearthed. Opposite the hospital and a few metres to the right, remains of the Hellenistic period were discovered, while a few metres further east a 5th c.B.C. temple has been unearthed. Undoubtedly we shall learn a lot more,

Polis - Street Map

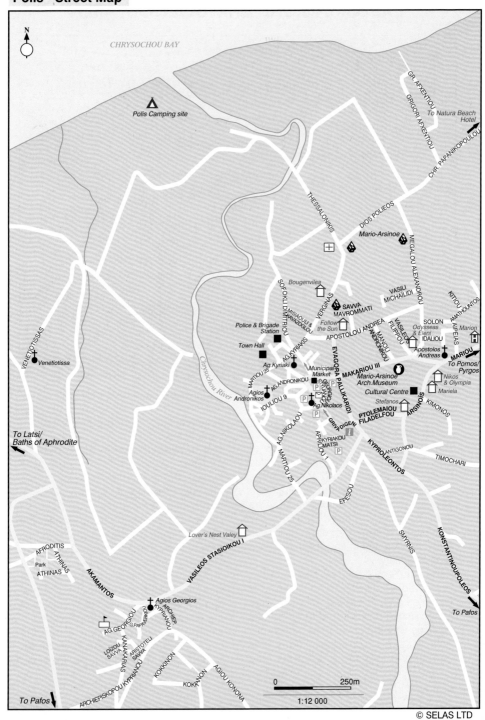

CHRYSOCHOU BAY

N

Polis Camping site

To Natura Beach
Hotel

GR. ΑΡΧΕΝΤΙΟΥ
ΓΡΙΓΟΡΗ ΑΡΧΕΝΤΙΟΥ
ΧΡ. ΠΑΠΑΝΙΚΟΠΟΥΛΟΥ

THESSALONIKIS
DIOS POLIEOS

Mario-Arsinoe

MEGALOU ALEXANDROU
KITIOU AIREIAS
AMATHOUNTOS

Bougenvilea

VASILI
MICHAILIDI

SOLON
Odysseas
& Eleni
IDALIOU

Marion

VERGINAS
SOFOKLI DIMITRIOU
MISIAOULI & KAVAZOGLOU

SAVVA
MAVROMMATI

Follow
the Sun

VASILEOS
FILIPPOU

MANOLI
ANDRONIKOU

Police & Brigade
Station

APOSTOLOU ANDREA

Apostolos †
Andreas

MARIOU

Town Hall

AG.KYRIAKIS

To Pomos/
Pyrgos

Ag.Kyriaki

Agios
Andronikos

MARTIOU 25

AG.ANDRONIKOU

IOULIOU 9

Municipal
Market

EVAGORA PALLIKARIDI

MAKARIOU III

Mario-Arsinoe
Arch.Museum

Nikos
& Olympia
Mariela

ARSINOIS
KIMONOS

Cultural Centre

Stefanos

Ag.Nikolaos

AG. NIKOLAOU

MARTIOU 25

GRIVA DIGENI

APRILIOU 1
KYRIAKOU
MATSI

PTOLEMAIOU
FILADELFOU

KYPROLEONTOS
ANTIGONOU
TIMOCHARI

To Latsi/
Baths of Aphrodite

Chrysochou River

EFESOU

SMYRNIS

KONSTANTINOUPOLEOS

Lover's Nest Valley

VASILEOS STASIOIKOU I

AFRODITIS
ATHINAS
Park
ATHINAS

AKAMANTOS

To Pafos

Agios Georgios

AG.GEORGIOU
ARCHIEP.
KYPRIANOU
G.PAPADOPOULOU

LOIZOU
SAVVA
KANAKARIAS
ARISTOTELI
SAVVA

KOKKINON

KOKKINON
AGIOU KONONA

ARCHIEPISKOPOU KYPRIANOU

To Pafos

Venetiotissa

VENETIOTISSAS

0   250m

1:12 000

including the line of the ancient wall of the town, as the excavations continue. The discovery of ancient Mario, the town's relations with the rest of the Greek world and the trade transactions of ancient Mario with Greece will throw light on the history of the town.

The elegant neoclassical building has already been completed along a central road and is now housing the rich archaeological finds of Mario-Arsinoe.

We cannot ignore historic sources for ancient Mario and Arsinoe. Skylakas characterises Mario as "a Greek town" and Stephanos Byzantios underlines that Arsinoe "was previously called Mario". Pliny defines Kinyras as the inventor of copper, and Mario is referred to as a copper centre. Perhaps the armour Kinyras gave to Agamemnon was made of copper produced near Mario. Today, to the east of Polis, left of the road to Limni, there is mine waste, an indication that copper was smelted in ancient times. Historians also mention that Mario was conquered in 449 B.C. by Kimon and that the last king of the town was Stasiikos II. Ptolemy demolished and destroyed the town because of its support to Antigonos, his opponent. King Stasiikos was killed and his subjects were transferred to Pafos in 312 B.C. Thus, on the foundations of ancient Mario, Arsinoe was later established.

With Christianity spreading in Cyprus, Arsinoe acquired a bishopric and, during Frankish times, the seat of the Bishopric was transferred here. Later, Polis and its fertile lands became a much-sought feud. Florio Bustron mentions that it was granted to Dame Mariette de Matres.

Recent archaeological work at the mosque of Polis, has revealed that the arched Byzantine church of St Andronikos, entirely painted with 15th and 16th c. paintings, was converted into a mosque immediately after the conquest of Cyprus by the Turks in 1571. The visitor can now observe and admire impressive paintings, on the walls which, until very recently, had been whitewashed by the Turks.

The central square of Polis has recently been renovated with paved limestone slabs, while the colourful tents outside the cafés, the restaurants and other shops attract tourists and passers-by.

To the north of Polis settlement, a remarkable **camping site** has been functioning since

Central Square of Polis

POLIS CAMPING

It is a category "A" camping site situated about 1 km from Polis, on the beach. It currently functions between March and October and can accommodate 200 caravans or tents. Total charges are €10 per tent or caravan including taxes and services. It is equipped with car parking, toilets, shower and washing facilities, piped drinking water, mini market, cafeteria/restaurant.

1980. It is one of the few camping sites in Cyprus, with a capacity of 250 caravans or tents and it can accommodate up to 750 people. It offers a number of facilities to te holiday-makers; enough shade for the caravans and tents, a parking place, a refreshment stand, a supplies shop, sanitation, games for children, a suitable road network and many more.

The beach next to the camping site has a width of about 20 metres and consists of small and large pebbles.

Chrysochou, a Turkish-Cypriot village, was originally Greek-Cypriot, as one can judge from the church turned into a mosque after the Turkish occupation in the 16th century.

Almost the entire land of Chrysochou is covered with a variety of plants such as tobacco, citrus, olive trees and some cereals.

Many authors mention Chrysochou, while Mas Latrie points out that the village was granted, as a feud, by Henry II to his cousin Hugo de Lousignan. During the Frankish occupation Chrysochou was the centre of one of the districts Cyprus was divided into. Even after the Turkish occupation of the island (1571 A.D.), when Cyprus was divided into katillikia (departments), Chrysochou continued to be the administrative seat of the area.

South-east of the village of Chrysochou, another Turkish village, **Karamoullides,** existed until 1975. Today a few refugees live in the village, occupied in dry-fed cropping.

It seems that the village existed even before the Turkish occupation of Cyprus in 1571, under the name Kalamoulli. Mas Latrie mentions it as a feud during the Frankish period.

Goudi is situated on the bank of Chrysochou river, about 6 km south of Polis Chrysochou, and enjoys a rare and boundless view towards Chrysochou valley and the villages south of Pafos forest.

The settlement consists of a mixture of modern and traditional houses.

A modern olive press serves not only the villagers but also the olive producers of the nearby villages. Mas Latrie mentions the village under the name Voudi and Vuti. He includes it in the list of Frankish royal estates belonging, with other villages, to Chrysochou region.

Built on the left bank of Chrysochou river, about 7 km south of Polis, **Choli** village enjoys a rare view extending towards almost all directions.

The village hosts some centuries-old olive trees as well as a rare traditional architecture. However, the visitor to the village looks mainly for the medieval church of Archangelos Michail, since the old church of the Virgin Mary is ruined. The church of Archangelos Michail, is a vaulted, single-aisled building that has recently been restored. The arch in the western section is taller than that of the main church. No evidence exists concerning the history of the village itself, or whether the church of Archangelos Michail was the chapel of a feudal lord. The frescoes, however, date from the 15th or the 16th century, even though a great number, probably the most representative ones, are damaged. The frescoes in the northern section of the church refer to the life of the Virgin Mary, with one row depicting Joachim and Anna. In the southern section they depict scenes from the New Testament. The Crucifixion is one of the best preserved frescoes, showing the Virgin and John in deep sorrow next to Crucified Christ.

On the Polis-Stroumpi road, just 6 km away from Polis, lies **Skoulli,** all green in natural and cultivated vegetation. The plane, poplar and maple trees abound next to the citrus trees, the tobacco and other cultivations. The church of Agios Kournoutas does not exist any more, but the place-name is well-known. However, the church of Agios Andronikos is well preserved. It is arched with two stone zones inside and an inscription that dates back to 1716, probably the date it was built or restored. Agios Andronikos is the last relic of Kerepin or Tzerapin, the settlement that disappeared during the last century.

Currently, Skoulli hosts the Reptiles Museum, which attracts a considerable number of visitors who come to Skoulli to see the reptiles of Cyprus.

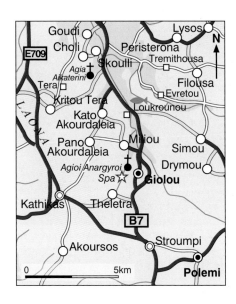

b) Hilly areas west of Chrysochou valley

> **Route: Kato Akourdaleia, Pano Akourdaleia, Loukrounou, Miliou, Agioi Anargyroi Monastery, Giolou**

Dissected, with a slope to the east, **Kato Akourdaleia,** is a village rich in traditional architecture. In the village's Museum of Folk Art are housed traditional treasures inherited from previous generations. The museum is worth visiting.

The church of Agia Paraskevi is of cruciform style with a dome, originally full of frescoes. It maintains its skylights and some worn out frescoes. Part of an icon which can be seen in the church may be quite old. In the village a tradition is preserved about Rigaina and Digenis. Digenis had his home at the locality "Digenies", while the Queen lived at Tsouvlitzin. When the church of Agia Aikaterini was being built, there was no water and the builders, according to tradition, made mud using milk. Digenis wished to marry Rigaina but she was not

Museum of Folk Art, Kato Akourdaleia

Tobacco cultivations in the Chrysochou valley

as Digenis' Rocks, are still to be found near the farm of Dkio Potamoi, next to the Baths of Aphrodite. The same story is told in Kritou Tera.

Pano Akourdaleia has a varied natural vegetation rich in terebinths and oak trees. The houses are traditional, built with hewn limestone blocks.

An earthen road connects Pano Akourdaleia with Kathikas and the rest of the Laona plateau. The damaged church of Panagia Chryseleousa, in the middle of the village, according to Gunnis, dates back to the 16th century. The church was originally full of frescoes but they are currently worn out.

The settlement of **Loukrounou,** on the west bank of the Chrysochou valley, is currently deserted.

North of Giolou and next to the Monastery of Agioi Anargyroi lies **Miliou.** Most of the houses are traditional, built with hewn limestone and surrounded by flowered gardens. Apart from the few inhabitants who are farmers, there are two well-established weavers. Some houses have been restored either to be used by the owners themselves or to be rented out. On one of the village slopes lie the remains of the medieval monastery of Agios Fotios. According to tradition, this Monastery had 70 monks, while Agioi Anargyroi Monastery was its annex. The three-aisled church was destroyed in 1934 along with all its frescoes.

West of the Chrysochou valley, between the villages of Giolou and Miliou, the visitor can find the **Monastery of Agioi Anargyroi,** built in 1649 and currently being the centre of a spa. The monastery of Agioi Anargyroi is one of the 79 monasteries mentioned by Kyprianos, most of which were functioning during the Turkish rule. The modern single-aisled, arched church, which has obviously been restored a number of times, maintains the original thick walls and some old, portable icons. The decline and final

interested and, in order to put him off, she asked for something which, according to her, was impossible: she asked him to dig a ditch from his residence so that water could be transferred to her home. Digenis dug the ditch but the Queen, in order to escape him, fled from her home and went to the bay of Chrysochou. Digenis is said to have thrown two rocks at her, which missed their target. These rocks known,

abandonment of the monastery must have come around the middle or towards the end of the 19th century. Kyriazis underlines that the Monastery was "quite rich and thriving during the early part of the 19th century". N. Clerides mentions the Bishop of Pafos, Iacovos Antzoulatos, who restored the Monastery in 1922 at the expense of the bishopric, adding new rooms. It was then that chemical tests were carried out on its sulphur waters and their therapeutic quality was discovered.

From the early part of the present century, Agioi Anargyroi was either used as a monastery or was hired out and used for therapeutic purposes. Until a few years ago it was used once again by nuns from Greece and Cyprus, but currently has been transformed into baths. It is not known how the Monastery came to be identified with the names of Agios Cosmas and Damianos, known as Agioi Anargyroi. According to tradition, they were brothers practising as doctors, who did not accept payment from their patients. Perhaps the therapeutic springs next to the monastery and the free treatment given to the patients explains the name it was given. Nevertheless, there is a myth about this monastery, widely spread among the inhabitants of the surrounding villages. According to this tradition, many years ago a number of monks lived in the monastery. One day they argued among themselves and they not only used sticks and stones in their dispute but also eggs from the cellar, because it was during the period of Lent. As a result of the argument, the eggs broke and the water from the springs took the smell of rotten eggs.

The tests carried out on the sulphur waters of the springs showed them to be effective for the treatment of bone problems, rheumatism, skin diseases and digestive disorders. Agioi Anargyroi baths can take up to 40 people, and the patients are mainly middle-aged, coming

Agioi Anargyroi Monastery, currently Agioi Anargyroi spa

not only from Cyprus but from abroad as well. Agioi Anargyroi is considered a one star hotel with ordinary as well as sulphurous water in each room. The residents can choose the water of their liking. Besides, a swimming pool has recently been set up in the garden of the hotel.

There are few villages in Cyprus and even fewer in the Pafos district, which, despite the distance from urban and tourist centres, have not only managed to retain their population but also to increase it. Such a village is **Giolou**, between Stroumpi and Polis.

The modern church of Chryseleousa is large. Built in a new architectural style, it is a jewel for the village. The old church, which bears the same name, built in the 18th century, contains an icon of the Virgin Mary which was painted in the 17th century. It is said that this icon was originally in the church of Peristerona village but a peasant from Giolou dreamt one night that the neighbouring village was on fire. He managed to save the icon which he brought to Giolou. This huge icon of the Virgin Mary is rain compelling, taken by farmers round the fields, in times of drought.

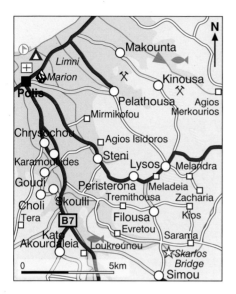

c) Hilly areas east of Chrysochou valley

> **Route: Mirmikofou, Agios Isidoros, Steni, Peristerona, Meladeia, Lysos, Agios Merkourios, Melandra, Zacharia, Filousa, Tremithousa, Kios, Sarama, Evretou.**

Mirmikofou had been a deserted settlement since the forties. Most probably Marmika, appearing on the Venetian maps, is Mirmikofou. Gunnis refers to a medieval church with mural paintings.

Agios Isidoros, north-west of Steni, is today an abandoned settlement. It is, however, a medieval settlement, as it appears on the Venetian maps under the name S.Sidro.

In a narrow location of the valley of Steni lies the settlement of **Steni** which obviously owes its name to its geographical position.

Though written witnesses of the medieval history of Steni are non-existent, nevertheless one cannot ignore the old monastery of Chrysolakourna, dating back to the

12th century and lying about three km north of the settlement. Exact details of the date the monastery was built are not known, though in 1821 it was considered a significant monastery. Tsiknopoullos mentions that Chrysolakourna was, at some time, the seat of the Bishop of Pafos.

It was abandoned in the 19th century but restored as a three-aisled basilica in 1974 and 1975. There are still a few worn-out frescoes like St John the Baptist dating back to the 12th century as well as Platytera amid the Angels, St George, etc.

Other noteworthy features are the scattered marble columns and capitals, the arches between the aisles and the impeccable carved limestone with which the church was constructed.

Tsiknopoullos, repeated by Kyriazis, mentions a miracle of the Madonna of Chrysolakourna. A few Saracens wanted to usurp the well of the monastery and in order to clean it one of them entered the well but died as he was beaten by an invisible hand. The same fate befell the second one. A third one was drawn to the surface half dead.

Peristerona, east of the Chrysochou valley, lies on a conspicuous location with an extensive view towards many directions.

Natural vegetation is rich and varied with Cyprus oak and Hermes oak trees predominating.

The history and archaeology of the village are still unknown. A few olive-presses and the old portable icons in the church of Agios Mamas, is what the visitor can see.

Meladeia, is an abandoned settlement, currently inhabited by a single shepherd. The village, however, was a royal estate during the Frankish period.

Lysos, close to Pafos forest, is rich in natural vegetation, particularly of pine,

Old monastery of Chrysolakourna (Steni)

oak, thyme, gorse, alder and plane trees.

Lysos is currently depopulated, with a large number of its inhabitants living in South Africa and other countries. In the past copper pyrite was extracted close by, an information passed on to us by Hogard and Gaundry, who underline the mining of copper ore near the village. Hogard writes about ancient tombs which probably belonged to miners.

Lysos has many churches, the most important of which is that of Panagia (Madonna) Chryseleousa. It is a restored edifice, which originally was probably a Latin church. Two coats of arms, above the north and south doors indicate the medieval age of the church. Jeffery concludes that at least one of the coats-of-arms belongs to the powerful family of Gourri.

The traditional stone-built fountain of the village with its outlets, the village square with the small artificial pool, the cultural centre where valuable artifacts of the village are housed, as well as the small park with its flowered garden, are special features of the village.

The folklore of the village is also remarkable. In the "plain" lies the "footstep", of Digenis, this legendary hero of Cyprus during the Middle Ages. Lysos and particularly the forest area east of Lysos has hosted a number of Cypriot fighters during the Liberation Struggle (1955-59), including the hanged hero, Evagoras Pallikarides. Recently a commemorative monument has been erected at the locality where he was seized.

Agios Merkourios, north-east of Lysos, is currently abandoned. Around 1949 the British Colonial Administration decided that the village should be removed elsewhere, as it was lying within the Pafos forest, the protection of which was indispensable.

Until recently, a forest station was functioning in Agios Merkourios. In hide-outs among the deep-sided valleys, the rough scenery and the dense forest cover, a number of Cypriot fighters stayed during the Liberation Struggle for Independence (1955-59).Close to the bridge of Agios

Lysos, Chryseleousa church

Merkourios the pictures are insuperable, with moufflons jumping and running before your eyes.

Melandra is an abandoned settlement, appearing on the Venetian maps as a medieval settlement. According to Gunnis, who mentions the two chapels of the village, Agios Theosevios, who was regarded as protector of farmers, was born in Melandra. His brother became bishop of Arsinoe and after his death was declared a saint.

Zacharia is an abandoned settlement south-east of Lysos. Kyriazis underlines that it probably obtained its name from a well-known noble Genoese family.

Filousa (Chrysochou), south of Lysos, enjoys an extensive view towards the valley of Stavros tis Psokas and the Evretou dam.

The village is at least medieval, since together with Evretou were feuds belonging to Pero Zerpas during the Frankish period.

Tremithousa is an abandoned settlement west of Filousa.

Instinjo (Kios) is an abandoned settlement, east of Filousa, appearing on Venetian maps as Kios.

Sarama is an abandoned settlement in the valley of Stavros tis Psokas. It was a royal estate during the Frankish period.

Evretou is a deserted settlement, on the bank of Stavros tis Psokas river. It is mentioned by Florio Bustron as a Frankish feud.

AGIOS MERKOURIOS PICNIC SITE

It is situated 7 km from Lysos to Stavros tis Psokas, 4 km on the forest road which leads to Agios Merkourios. It has a capacity of 30 persons. It is equipped with car parking, toilets, piped drinking water, tables and benches, barbecue facilities and children's play areas.

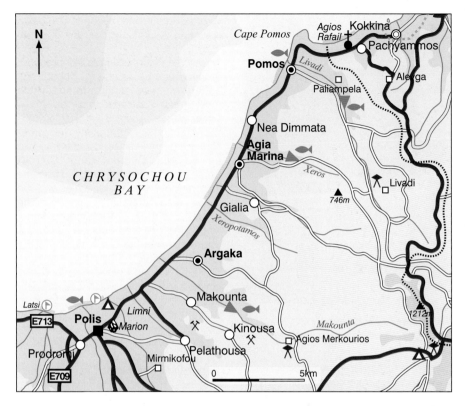

d) Coastal plain east of Chrysochou

Route: Pelathousa, Makounta, Kinousa, Limni Mines, Argaka, Gialia, Agia Marina, Nea Dimmata, Pomos, Livadi, Paliampela

Pelathousa lies south-east of Polis, where once extended the Limni mines. In the middle of the sparsely populated settlement stands the mosque of the village with its tall minaret. The church of Agia Aikaterini was converted to mosque, after the conquest of Cyprus by the Turks in 1571. Continued white washing has worn out possible mural paintings.

Pelathousa appears on Venetian maps, while Hogard writes about ancient tombs which probably belonged to miners. Worth visiting is the church of Panagia (Madonna) Horteri, about three kilometres outside the village. It is a single-aisled, domed, Byzantine building, originally painted. Currently, only traces of the original mural paintings are preserved. North of the church there was probably another aisle. The church of Panagia Horteri belongs, most probably to the 14th or 15th century.

The road to **Makounta,** between Polis and Argaka, passes through the mine-waste of the Limni mines.

The old chapel of Agios Georgios, close to the dam, does not exist any more. Instead a modern chapel has been built in the same locality. Makounta is a medieval settlement appearing on Venetian maps.

Kinousa, close to Pafos forest, is known for its two mines of copper pyrites. The

Pelathousa minaret constructed on a Christian church

Traditional chair-making, Kinousa

Cyprus Sulphur and Copper Company, stationed at Limni, worked the ore from 1951 till 1960.

Traditional chair-making is still practised in the village by an artisan. Hogard and Jeffery mention ancient tombs which most probably belonged to miners.

Limni Mines. About 5 km east of Polis there are still remains of the once-flourishing Limni mining company, known as Cyprus Sulphur and Copper Company. The ore was exported from the little harbour with its long pier and the surrounding installations. Apart from the Limni mine there is the Kinousa mine, where the ore was dug out using the open-cast method. Also nearby is the Evlogimeni mine.

The area around Polis-Limni-Kinousa is covered with scoriae which probably date back to the Bronze era or at least to Roman times. Nearby is the site of the ancient Mario mine, where copper was produced and exported. Most probably the armour Kinyras gave to Agamemnon, as mentioned by Homer, was produced from copper extracted from Mario mine.

The modern works date back to 1882, and continued uninterrupted until 1920. The production of copper began in 1937 and continued until 1979, when the mine was closed after the reserves were exhausted. Copper was not the only ore which was dug out from Limni. There was also gold, silver and sulphur.

Argaka. Despite the fact that there are two villages, known as Kato and Pano Argaka, nevertheless, officially there is only one Argaka, about two km east of the coast. There is no record of the origins of the village, or whether it existed during medieval times. Nevertheless, east of the village lies the restored church of Agia Varvara with its carved doors and a few capitals belonging to an old monastery. In July 1821 the abbot of the monastery martyred together with other national heroes. Kyriazis also notes that

Agia Varvara belonged to the Jerusalem Patriarchate and functioned until 1821, having an abbot and two monks. Near the church is the monastery's holy well, known as Vrysin tou Kalogirou (The Monk's well), because Abbot Sofronios was known as "The Monk". Perhaps the monastery of Agia Varvara is the nucleus of today's Argaka.

Gialia is on the coastal road after Argaka village and is divided into Pano and Kato Gialia, even though there is really only one Gialia. Gialia is known for its tasty oranges.

The settlement extends down the valley, mainly along two parallel roads, north and south of the river to a distance of 3,5 km. This is one of the most classical linear-type settlements of Cyprus.

Florio Bustron gives the names Lallia, Laglia and Gialia to the village. He also mentions the monastery of Gialia. Besides, Gunnis refer to the monastery of Agios Kournoutas, "about two miles east of the village". As has been suggested, it could have been a Latin building.

The Georgian professor Djobadje found remains of the Gialia monastery in 1981, along with evidence that it belonged to Georgian monks who lived in Cyprus. Neither the foundation nor the disappearance date of the monastery are known. Perhaps the monastery belongs to the 13th century. Georgios Voustronios also refers to the monastery existing in 1460 during the Frankish rule. The village has a Greek name, Egialia, which with the passing of time became Gialia.

Agia Marina settlement near the coast is recent. The original settlement to the east, near the forest, was abandoned. The dam constructed recently and the irrigation of a vast area of land transformed the agricultural economy of the village.

Nea Dimmata is a new settlement, established at the beginning of the 1950's by the British Government so that its inhabitants, mainly stock-breeders and

Makounta, local cheese-making

Apricot -production, Nea Dimmata

lumbermen, could be transferred from the forest to the west. The church of Profitis Ilias stands on a prominent spot, near the sea, while recently a number of new buildings are being constructed along the road between Polis-Pomos. The land slopes towards the sea, and the coastal formations, particularly capes and sandy bays, are very impressive.

Agia Marina dam

Pomos. The route from Nea Dimmata to Cape Pomos is one of the most picturesque coastal routes of Cyprus. The mountains fall vertically to the sea, while their slopes are covered with pine trees. The coastline is laced, while the sea water has a dark-blue colour.

Currently, there is tourist development in the village, evidenced by the country houses scattered around the area, and the rooms to be let to summer visitors. There are also restaurants and their business is augmented by the number of pilgrims to the church of Agios Raphael, in Pachyammos.

Pomos' fishing harbour is picturesque and allows a number of boats to carry on their fishing activities. Cape Pomos is often referred to as Kallinousa, Agia Eleni, Alexandretta etc, which requires archaeological investigation. East of the village is the arched Chrysopateritissa church, with a raised narthex. According to Gunnis, it dates from the 16th century, although the actual narthex was built in 1816. There is a worn-out icon of the Virgin Mary Chrysopateritissa painted in 1524. Also on the north exterior door is an inscription.

Livadi, by the river bank of Livadi river, is currently abandoned, since the colonial govenment as from 1954 transferred the settlement to Morfou area.

A picnic site has recently been set up at Livadi.

Paliampela is an abandoned settlement in Tillyria, on the banks of the Livadi river, east of Pomos.

GEFYRI TOU LIVADIOU PICNIC SITE

It is situated 13 km south of Pomos towards Stavros tis Psokas Forest Station. It has a capacity of 270 persons. It is equipped with car parking, toilets, piped drinking water, tables and benches, barbecue facilities and children's play areas.

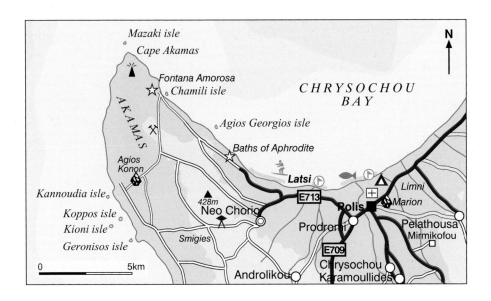

Map of the Akamas peninsula and Chrysochou Bay showing: Mazaki isle, Cape Akamas, Fontana Amorosa, Chamili isle, Agios Georgios isle, Baths of Aphrodite, Latsi, Agios Konon, Kannoudia isle, Koppos isle, Kioni isle, Geronisos isle, Neo Chorio (428m), Smigies, Androlikou, Polis, Prodromi, Limni, Marion, Pelathousa, Mirmikofou, Chrysochou, Karamoullides, CHRYSOCHOU BAY. Scale 0–5km. Routes E713, E709.

e) Coastal plain West of Chrysochou

Route: Prodromi, Latsi, Neo Chorio

Prodromi is no longer an independent settlement but a suburb of the ever-expanding Polis, falling within its municipality boundaries.

The village does not depend any more on farming, since the tourist trade began and has continued to develop. Hotels and tourist apartments are being built and tavernas are being set up, as are supermarkets and other tourist services.

In an effort to beautify the village and its surroundings, the original fountain close to the centre of the village, has been restored. The old water-mill next to the Chrysochou river is a relic of the previous century.

The church of Venethkiotissa, now on the administrative boundaries of Prodromi-Polis, is possibly medieval. Only the foundations of the ancient church have survived, since the building has been completely renovated. The picturesque harbour of **Latsi** has a horseshoe shape, with two stone jetties, flanked by two small lighthouses with a wooden pier about 45 metres long towards the centre. Dozens of fishing boats, small and large, are moored in the harbour and various coloured bags containing fishing nets are almost always lined up on the jetty. A number of fishermen with their assistants start off from here in the afternoon, when there is no moon, or at midnight with the moonlight, so that they can fish up to cape Akamas, or even further afield to Kioni, up to cape Pomos or even towards Rhodes, when in search for swordfish.

Very rarely do ships dock here now. In the past they would come to the harbour and empty their holds of wheat and barley and load up with carobs.

This "black gold" was kept in huge warehouses which belonged to various traders and were used by all the producers. This was particularly evident during the first decades of this century, when carobs were a very valuable product for export purposes.

Pomos coastline

West of the bay, there are the remains of an old construction which obviously pre-existed the jetty found there today. Even if the wooden jetty was put up during the British rule, the old jetty dates to the Turkish occupation, or even from previous historical eras.

Currently, the carob warehouses have been turned into restaurants and hotels. The beach to the west of the harbour has become a sought-after swimming area. Furthermore, Latsi has a Diving School for those who wish to learn or exercise. Special boats from Latsi can take the tourists on a tour round the beautiful Akamas beaches up to Fontana Amorosa and even further on.

Elia Latsi Holiday Village is a unique holiday resort with all amenities comprising many features of traditional architecture. It houses an archaeological museum with samples from all historical periods of Cyprus.

Neo Chorio lies on a hilltop enjoying a wonderful view of Chrysochou bay with a relatively easy approach to Akamas forest from the west. A great part of Akamas is included in the administrative boundaries of Neo Chorio. The coastline consists of cliffs and beaches of sand and pebble.

In its administrative area lie Latsi, with the surrounding sandy or pebbled beaches, the Baths of Aphrodite, Dyo Potamoi, the islets, Agios Minas, Fontana Amorosa, Pyrgos tis Rigainas, Smygies, and much more. There are a number of abandoned churches, a deserted forestry station, while the magnesium and black earth extraction is almost forgotten.

The area's folklore is remarkable, with the legends of Digenis and Rigaina. At the Baths of Aphrodite the goddess would bathe and cleanse her body from the salty waters of the neighbouring sea. This is where Adonis first laid eyes on her. Further on lies the Spring of Eros,

Daily trips to Akamas from Latsi

Amateur fishing, Latsi

View close to the Baths of Aphrodite

Fontana Amorosa, which Ariosto describes in his lovely verses:

"Nowhere else in the world have I seen women and virgins so lovely and attractive".

In a great ravine, near the Baths of Aphrodite, there is a cave engraved in the rock (Spilios tis Rigainas). This is where, the Queen would hide away after every bath she had.

Also, near the Baths of Aphrodite, there are two rocks in the sea that Digenis threw in an attempt to prevent the Queen escaping from him, when she ignored a promise she had given to him. From then on the two rocks were named "Rocks of Digenis".

Neo Chorio caters for tourists not only within the settlement but also near the beaches. Its beaches are full of sunbathers in the summer and a number of Cypriot campers stay beneath the carob trees during the months of July and August. Beween Latsi and the Baths of Aphrodite there are many small and large beaches, which can satisfy every taste.

In the administrative area of Neo Chorio, remarkable underground caves with superb stalactites and stalagmites have recently been discovered. Entry to the underground world of Neo Chorio is not currently possible.

AVAILABLE IN LATSI

Bank

Diving Centre

Fishing shelter

Hotel/Tourist Apts

Restaurant

THE NORTH-WESTERN PART OF PAFOS DISTRICT

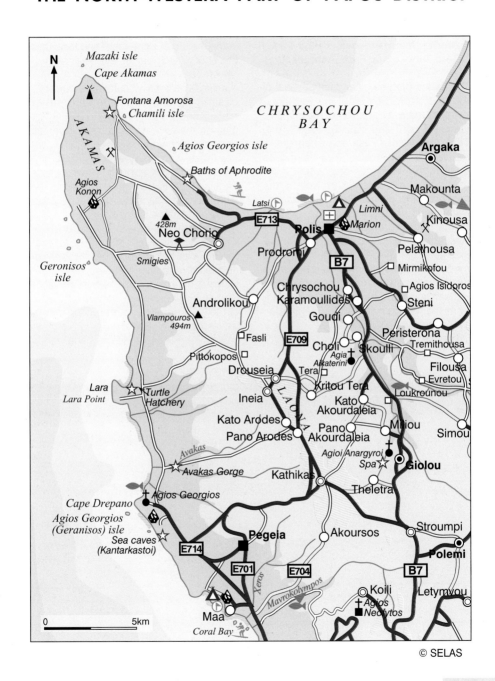

N

Mazaki isle
Cape Akamas

Fontana Amorosa
Chamili isle

CHRYSOCHOU BAY

Agios Georgios isle

Argaka

A K A M A S

Baths of Aphrodite

Makounta

Agios Konon

Latsi

Limni

Kinousa

E713

428m
Neo Chorio

Polis

Marion

Pelathousa

Prodromi

Smigies

B7

Mirmikofou

Agios Isidoros

Geronisos isle

Androlikou

Chrysochou
Karamoullides

Steni

Goudi

Peristerona

Vlampouros
494m

Fasli

E709

Choli

Tremithousa

Skoulli

Pittokopos

Agia
Aikaterini

Filousa

Drouseia

Tera

Evretou

Lara
Lara Point

Turtle
Hatchery

Ineia

Kritou Tera

Loukrounou

Kato
Akourdaleia

Kato Arodes

Pano
Akourdaleia

Miliou

Simou

Pano Arodes

Avakas

Agioi Anargyroi
Spa

Giolou

Avakas Gorge

Kathikas

Theletra

Cape Drepano

Agios Georgios

Agios Georgios
(Geranisos) isle

Sea caves
(Kantarkastoi)

Pegeia

Akoursos

Stroumpi

E714

Polemi

E701

E704

B7

Koili

Letymvou

Agios
Neofytos

Xeros

Mavrokolympos

Maa

Coral Bay

0   5km

© SELAS

a) The Laona villages

Route: Kathikas, Akoursos, Theletra, Pano Arodes, Avakas Gorge, Kato Arodes, Ineia, Drouseia, Kritou Tera, Tera, Pittokopos, Fasli, Androlikou

The **Laona plateau** extends south-east of Akamas, from Stroumpi via Kathikas, Arodes, Ineia, Drouseia to Neo Chorio (southern part) and includes Kritou Tera, Tera, Androlikou, Fasli and Akoursos. It reaches a height of 670 m having as frontiers the valley of Chrysochou to the east and Akamas forest as well as the narrow coastal plain of Pafos, to the west.

Kathikas is situated in the southern part of the Laona plateau, surrounded by vineyards, which constitute the principal income of the village. Though there is no evidence that Kathikas existed as a medieval settlement, nevertheless Hellenistic tombs have been unearthed, while the well-known circular Roman road passed through the village.

The wines of Kathikas were known for their taste. Among those who extolled Kathikas wines was Gaudry, in 1855, who wrote that the village produced "excellent red wines". The gathering of grapes starts in the middle of September and lasts until the end of October or the beginning of November.

Kathikas, besides viticulture, is currently casting its glance to tourism, either renting houses to tourists or catering for them in the form of restaurants, tavernas and small supermarkets.

For those who enjoy walking there is a nature trail 1 km from Kathikas towards Pegeia, near "Kyparissos" restaurant. The length of the trail is approximately 2 km and the walk time is one hour.

Akoursos, a small village, south of Kathikas, engaged mainly in animal raising, can be visited either through an asphalted road lying between Kisonerga-Pegeia or via an earthen road from Kathikas. The village belonged to the Grand Commandery, though it might have been a Byzantine or earlier settlement. Probably the most noteworthy

Loading grapes on lorries

Kathikas Nature Trail

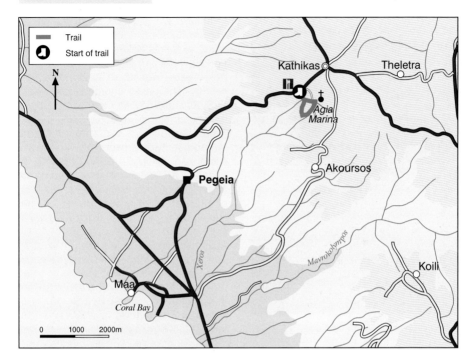

feature is a hollow on a vertical cliff close to the village. The hollow looks like the encleistra of Agios Neofytos. According to tradition, the cave communicates with two others in which frescoes of Agioi Konstantinos and Eleni can be seen. It is an extremely vertical cliff presenting problems for exploration.

Theletra can be approached either through the Stroumpi-Polis road or via the new asphalted road from Kathikas. The old settlement, at the base of a cliff, preserves its charm with its limestone-built houses, the arched two-storeyed houses and its meandering streets. The landslides were the main reason for Theletra's removal to a new location on a flat surface, not far away. The modern settlement, as it is obvious, is planned with the uniform houses arrayed on both sides of the roads.

Besides, the old church of Panagia (Madonna) Chryseleousa, a building of 1755, contains a few old portable icons like that of Christ of 1528 and Panagia Theletrofylaktria of the 16th century.

The villagers often call their settlement Nea (New) Theletra to differentiate it from the old settlement, now abandoned.

Pano Arodes lies in the middle of the Laona plateau with an abundant view to the west as well as to the east. The varied rocks have affected the village's topography with the formation of spectacular gorges, karst phenomena and undulating chalky vineyards. The main agricultural product is grapes, particularly the white variety. An old wine-press, established on a limestone outcrop in the middle of a vine-producing area, is still preserved, constituting a site of interest.

Grape harvest

The village, judging from the archaeological findings, dates back to the Mycenean era. The settlement lies on an ancient necropolis. Leontios Machairas refers to Saints Kalandion, Agapios and Varlaam, Alaman saints, who settled in the village possibly during the 9th century. The parish church is dedicated to St Kalandion, while north and south of the church stand two sarcophagi, that of Agios Agapitikos and that of Agios Misitikos. Most probably the two sarcophagi belong to St Agapios and St Varlaam. A tradition exists according to which if somebody wishes to win the love or the hatred of a person, he or she should come secretly at night and chip a tiny fragment of the sarcophagus of Agios Agapitikos or Agios Misitikos. It is later powdered and introduced into the drink of the person one wishes to love or hate. It is said that there will always be an immediate response to the donor's feelings. The legend is well known in almost all Cyprus and even in some

Agios Agapitikos sarcophagus, Pano Arodes

Women on their way to the olive-mill (Arodes)

countries abroad. A few persons write and request some powder from the sacred monuments. This, according to tradition, is not permissible, nor does it produce any results. A personal visit is indespensable. The holy well of St Kalandion, a kilometre outside the village, in a pleasant and quiet environment, has recently been restored. The water is miraculous for skin diseases.

In between Arodes and Kathikas stands a conspicuous hill, called Vikla, from the Latin word which means observatory. From here the view to the sea, to the west, the gulf of Chrysochou to the north and the forest of Pafos to the east is insuperable. Most probably during the Byzantine period the hill acted as an observation point, with a tower which had later been demolished.

About three kilometres east of Pano Arodes lies the chapel of Panagia (Madonna) Chrysospiliotissa. There is a modern chapel built in 1947, restored in 1993, and an underground Roman tomb below the limestone outcrop, which later was transformed to a church with mural paintings. Currently, only traces of frescoes exist. The chapel is most probably the last remnant of the old settlement of Themokrini, appearing on many Venetian maps and cited by Mas Latrie as a royal estate during the Frankish period. It is also cited by Florio Bustron as a royal estate between 1383 and 1385. A beautiful folk poem is still preserved in the village concerning a very pretty girl, daughter of Themokrini's priest, who was seized by the Trurks to be transported to the Sultan's harem in Constantinople. The area around the chapel has recently been renovated and is currently furnished with drinking water and benches for the visitors. West of Arodes, stands the ancient monastery of Agios Savvas, now ruined. At the locality Lipati, west of Arodes, on the way to the Avakas gorge, there existed an ancient settlement, still waiting the archaeological spade.

There are quite a few cultural monuments in the village which the visitor can see, by following the good road network, recently established by land consolidation. Since

Donkeys still used in Laona

1995, Akamiron company in collaboration with Swiss specialists set up a laboratory in the village which produces sun remedies, disposed throughout the world. A visit to the laboratory is recommended.

The Avakas Gorge. The Avakas river starts in Arodes and ends up to the sea at Toxeftra. The gorge, however, is about two kilometres long originating at Koloni, west of Arodes settlement and ending up in Toxeftra. The gorge is the combined product of valley deepening, the rising of the land in relation to the sea and the subsequent rejuvenation of the river system by vertically deepening the pre-existing river valley.

If a visitor wishes to explore the two km gorge, walking is recommended from Koloni (Arodes). If, however, one wishes to see the mouth of the gorge only, then the visit can be accomplished from Toxeftra in Pegeia, near the sea. Exploring the gorge from Arodes, one can walk along the deep, steep-sided valley with cliffs on both sides, somewhere reaching the height of almost a hundred metres. Huge rocks, dropped from the sides, blocked the valley, while elsewhere the water of the stream disappears to reappear further west.

You encounter arches and caves, while some hollows on the bed fill with water even in summer. There is a rich variety of flora, like poplar, cypress, wild carobs and olive trees, lentisk, gorse, terebinth, thyme, rockrose, bramble and oleander. The fauna consists of foxes, wild pigeons, partridges, a few hares and other emigratory or endemic birds. A few night birds and some serpents are also present. In the past vultures lived on the steep limestone cliffs, but have now abandoned the place. Suitable boots are required as well as a camera. The exploration of the gorge is not recommended in winter months when the river is impassable. The awe and mystery that accompany the passage of the gorge, make the exploration very challenging.

Kato Arodes has a dissected topography, caused by Avakas and its streams, with the rounded chalky hills predominating. Until 1975 it was inhabited by Turkish Cypriots who relied on dry-fed crops.

Most probably until the Venetian period Kato Arodes was lying where Kato Aroa (place-name) exists today, west of Kato Arodes. The settlement was abandoned and a new one was set up exactly where currently Kato Arodes lies. In the early 1950's a winery was set up in Kato Arodes which ceased to function a few years later. Currently, only a few refugee families live in Kato Arodes, while the decision of the Government to restore some houses and use them for holiday-making, has attracted quite a few Cypriots to the settlement as early as 1993.

Ineia. Inside the settlement of Ineia there is not much to see apart from the traditional architecture with the limestone-built houses housing a relatively dense population. The view from the village, especially from the hill of St George, (670 m. a.s.l.) is boundless. According to

Karavopetres, Ineia

Jeffery, an observatory existed here in the 16th century.

The village of Ineia, belonged to the Grand Commandery which had its headquarters at Kolossi. Near the sea, stock-breeders from Ineia, exercising transhumance, set up, in the past, makeshift dwellings to satisfy their needs in winter, when they used to move to warmer coastal areas.

Close to their makeshift dwellings stand the well-known "Karavopetres", which are tall, isolated rocks in the sea close to the coast. It is here that pirates, during the Arab raids, moored their boats before looting, burning and destroying villages, monasteries and chapels. According to tradition, close to "Karavopetres", stood the monastery of Vlou (Tyflou). Currently, only a chapel stands at the place of the old monastery. When the monastery was looted and utterly destroyed by the corsairs, Madonna, according to tradition, not tolerating the contempt, transformed the ships into rocks which now stand fossilized in the sea.

The well known Lara "salt-lake", which, in essence, is a rocky surface with hollows filled with salty water in winter, lies in the administrative area of Ineia.

The isolated unique beaches of Lara, (Lara and Ammoudi) attract swimmers in summer who defy the dusty earthen road from Agios Georgios (Pegeia) or Ineia up to Lara. A **turtle hatchery** has been set up in Ammoudi a few years ago.

Drouseia, with its administrative boundaries reaching the Chrysochou valley to the east and the coastline of Akamas to the west, is rich on physical and cultural landforms and monuments. Few huge rocks of past geological eras are scattered in its landscape. The traditional architecture is very rich with elongated rooms, arched, two-storeyed houses, narrow meandering cobbled streets, carved doors and windows made of wood and so on. A few old peasants still wear traditional "vraka" (baggy breeches), while among the village craftsmen is a coppersmith.

At Kioni, in the Akamas area, a tiny portion of a pillar projecting above the sea-water, probably a relic of an ancient monument, is worth observing. Most probably the locality Kioni was the outport of the ancient city of Agios Konon, if not of ancient Akamantis. The church of Agios Konon built on the foundations of an ancient church with abundant water gushing forth from a spring nearby, and the holy well close by are a testimony of the old famous church. According to Gunnis, behind Agios Konon church lies a Hellenistic-Roman necropolis. All the region around is full of thrills. As many as 101 churches used to function in the region of Akamas.

On the eastern side of Drouseia lies the ancient monastery of Agios Georgios Nikoxylitis, surrounded by abundant greenery, particularly tall cypress-trees. The cells are ruined, while the arched dome of the church with its carved relief is preserved. Some portable icons have been transported to the parish church of Drouseia. It is not known when the monastery was built, but most probably it dates back to the 15th century. In 1923 it was destroyed by fire and since then rebuilt.

The recently-built hotel of Drouseia, gives the opportunity to both Cypriots and foreigners alike to acquaint themselves with the rich and varied physical and cultural heritage of the village.

Kritou Tera lies on a rocky surface sloping towards Chrysochou valley.

In the past people improved their income by engaging themselves in artistic and handicraft activities, like chair-making, saddle-making etc. Carob honey sweets, often covered with sesame, are a prerogative of the village.

Dragoman Hadjigeorgakis Kornesios, known as a distinguished Cypriot personality of the end of the 18th and the beginning of the 19th century, was born in Kritou Tera. His family house still exists, while the church of Chryseleousa, built by Kornesios at the beginning of the 19th century, is currently the parish church of the community. He acquired strength, even during the Turkish times, something despised by the ruling Turkish class. As Frangoudis cites, his strength was such that "with the Archbishop of Cyprus he was a second ethnarch, because without him, nothing could be imposed on the Christians". He was exiled by the Turks to Porte and subsequently beheaded in 1808. His mansion in Nicosia is currently a unique monument of interest. In Kritou Tera is preserved the first casino of Cypurs, a two-storeyed building with an arch, now declared an ancient monument. The casino was a coffe-shop where cards and gambling was its principal activity. Dancers from abroad, particularly from Smyrni and Adana entertained the players. The few paintings preserved, most probably belong to the last century.

Church of old monastery (Agios Georgios Nikoxylitis)

AVAILABLE IN DROUSEIA
Co-operative Credit Society
Folk Art Museum
Forest station
Hotel/Hotel Apts
Restaurant/Coffee shop

North-east of Kritou Tera stands the church of Agia Aikaterini, (Fytefkeias), a pole of attraction for many visitors. It is a three-aisled, Franco-Byzantine church, with a dome on the central aisle. The arches separating the aisle stand on bulky bases. Originally the church was painted throughout particularly in the interior. Currently, only some traces of the original mural paintings are preserved. The church has recently been renovated.

According to tradition, the flat land around the church of Agia Aikaterini, known as Fytefkeia, constituted a chiftlick which belonged to Rigaina (Queen). Numerous flocks were grazing in this large estate of the Queen. It is said that when the church of Agia Aikaterini was

The church of Agia Aikaterini

being built, because of the shortage of water, the builders used milk obtained from the sheep. Close by was the mansion of Digenis (the King) who was fascinated by the beauty of the Queen, whom she wanted as wife. Rigaina in order to escape him asked him to provide her with water-something unachievable-before marrying him. Digenis, after lengthy toils, opened a ditch and transported water to the villa of Rigaina. Rigaina who did not want to get married to Digenis, left the place, while the angry Digenis threw two huge blocks of rock against her, now lying in the sea, west of Latsi, known as "The Rocks of Digenis", close to the Baths of Aphrodite.

In the village a different version with Agia Aikaterini in the place of Rigaina, is prevalent. The traditional fountain with six outlets and the relics of some old water-mills are some additional sites of interest.

North and close to Kritou Tera, lies the deserted Turkish Cypriot settlement of **Tera.** It is remarkable that in the environs of Tera, a milestone of the Roman road connecting Pafos to Mario (Polis) was found. The village existed long before the conquest of Cyprus by the Turks in 1571.

A few inhabitants from nearby settlements, set up the hamlet of **Pittokopos,** lying off the road Drouseia-Fasli. The settlement, administratively belongs to Drouseia and comprises 5-6 houses with only two families currently living in them.

Fasli, an abandoned settlement, north-west of Drouseia, was, prior to 1975, a stock-breeding village with less than a hundred souls.

Until 1975, the Turkish-Cypriot community of **Androlikou** based its economy on animal raising, particularly sheep-rearing as well as dry-fed crops.

The radial morphology of the settlement is almost unique in Cyprus. From the centre of the village, where the mosque stands, six streets radiate to all directions. As Gunnis writes, the mosque "is built on the site of the church of St Andronikos".

A unique view of eastern Akamas coastline

b) The Akamas Region

Akamas, situated to the extreme north-west part of Pafos, often referred to as Akamas peninsula, is a rugged, wild and attractive area with unspoilt beaches and rocky coastline. Its flora is undisturbed with some rare plant species. However, Akamas is not simply a natural region with special geology, geomorphology and natural vegetation, but a very interesting cultural region as well with a history dating back to a few thousand years. This pristine area, where man lived since the Chalcolithic period, has been frequently looted and attacked by Arab raids, particularly in the seventh century A.D., a fact which forced the local inhabitants to move inland leaving behind villages, hamlets and chapels.

Unfortunately the northern part of Akamas is still a live firing range used by the British Forces. The visitors are requested to read the signposts and avoid visits during military exercises.

Akamas together with the forest of Pafos, particularly Stavros tis Psokas, are popular destinations for tourists, particularly those seeking tranquility and peace as well as scientists (botanists, geographers, geologists, ornithologists, etc), not excluding artists and writers. Furthermore, Akamas is a stopover place for millions of migratory birds on their route from Europe to Africa and vice versa.

Recently a number of foreign visitors explore Akamas through its nature trails.

There are many interpretations concerning the etymology of Akamas, the most prevalent of which is that of Akamas, the son of Theseus, who arrived in Cyprus after the Trojan war and founded Akamantis, a town in the Akamas region, still unearthed.

The true Akamas is the Forest of Akamas in the extreme north-western part of Pafos. Sometimes, erroneously, the term "Broader Akamas" is used, comprising Laona plateau, part of the northern coastal plain of Pafos, part of the western coastal plain of Chrysochou and often part of the valley of Chrysochou.

Geology

The geology of Akamas is rather complex, while the rocks are quite varied.In fact in Akamas the visitor finds rocks of the Ophiolithic complex of Troodos, a large variety of sedimentary rocks as well as rocks of the Mamonia Complex. The ridge of the peninsula coincides with serpentinised rocks fringed on the west by gabbros, plagiogranites as well as diabase. Further west, lavas, mainly basalts, even not continuous, occupy a significant part of the peninsula. The most significant sedimentary rocks are the reef limestones, particularly on the Lara "salt lake", a few bentonites and sandstones of Kannaviou formation, the limestones of Koronia, gravels and sands on the terraced beaches and a few alluvium deposits. Terrace deposits, though interrupted, extend from Lara to the cape of Akamas.

However, the Mamonia complex is the most interesting feature of the geology of Akamas. They are allochthonous igneous and sedimentary rocks of an unknown age. The most important of these rocks are thin bedded radiolarian cherts, siltstones, mudstones, limestones, calcarenites, guartzitic sandstones and grey-green sandstones with fossil remains. Besides, a few metamorphic rocks can be found close to the Baths of Aphrodite, consisting of schists, quartzite red phyllites, marbles etc. The specialists who visit Akamas are more interested in the ophiolithic complex of the region which, in essence, is a miniature of the ophiolithic complex of Troodos. However, the relationship of these two complexes is not yet abundantly clear.

Minerals

Magnesite is one of the ores that were extracted and exported about 75 years ago. Magnesia is the locality of the abandoned mine. The visitor can still see shafts and kilns where in the past a mining activity was thriving.

Copper and iron deposits are present in the peninsula of Akamas, though not sufficient to be exploited. Most of the bentonitic deposits are situated outside the true Akamas region, while marbles are limited in quantity. Even reef limestone, of exceptional quality, lies to the east of the region, in the area of Androlikou. Besides, "black earth" was also extracted and exported abroad a few decades ago.

Scenery and Landscape

The geology of Akamas, particularly the presence of a large variety of rocks as well as their structure, has greatly affected the scenery of Akamas.

In fact a ridge with a NW-SE direction divides the peninsula of Akamas, particularly the Forest of Akamas, into two parts with a number of streams flowing west. This ridge coincides with an anticline following the same direction. Relief reaches 494 m at Vlambouros, NW of Fasli and 428 at Mavri Shinia, north of Smigies. On account of the streams which dissect the landscape to the west a number of tiny deep valleys and gorges have been formed, while marine terraces, though narrow, have been formed, currently followed by an earthen road. The same marine terraces appear to the east reaching the Baths of Aphrodite. Akamas without a road network is considered to be the most pristine and inaccessible region of Cyprus. Only special cars can cross it.

Weather and climate

Though precise climatic data of Akamas are not available, nevertheless data of neighbouring stations permit a relatively true picture of the rainfall and temperatures prevailing in the region. The annual rainfall of Akamas is not much different from that of the whole of Cyprus which is 489 mm. At Polis it is 484 mm and at Pegeia 477, while

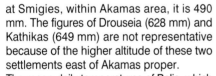

Cyclamen persicum

Centaurea akamantis
(Ph. courtesy of the Dep. of Forests)

at Smigies, within Akamas area, it is 490 mm. The figures of Drouseia (628 mm) and Kathikas (649 mm) are not representative because of the higher altitude of these two settlements east of Akamas proper.

The mean daily temperatures of Polis, which cannot be much different from Akamas, are quite high for winter as well as summer. In January temperature reaches 11,8 C and in July 26,6 C. Mean monthly max. temperature in January is 19,9 C and in July 37,5 C. The maquis type of vegetation prevailing in Akamas, though not original, is representative of the whole of Cyprus. It is because of the relatively high temperatures prevailing in summer as well as the winds from the west, particularly the frequent strong winds, that fires can be very serious, if not catastrophic, for the entire of Akamas. This is a reason why roads are needed to avoid possible disaster of the region.

Flora

Though there are three types of vegetation in Akamas (the pine forest, the garrique and the maquis), the maquis or thorny scrub growing to about two metres high is the most prevalent and most representative. It could be said that the maquis of Akamas is the most representative of Cyprus as a whole.

In Akamas there is a large variety of plants mainly because of the undisturbed nature of the region and because of the diversified scenery (rock faces, gorges, spring valleys, water courses, sand dunes etc.) Apart from the pines, the junipers, the wild olive and carob trees there are golden oaks, Hermes oaks, terebinths, lentiscs and particularly the unique strawberry tree (Arbutus unedo) which so far has been located only in Akamas. Rockrose with its rose and white flowers as well as gorse are abundant.

117

Serapias vomeracea
(Ph. courtesy of P. Christodoulou)

Besides, there is a score of endemic species which grow in Akamas alone. The Cyprus tulip, various types of anemones, cyclamens, a variety of orchids, the yellow everlasting ("athanato") the sea lavender, the tall asphodel, grape hyacinth, the star of Bethlehem, sand lilies, a variety of herbs such as sage, thyme, myrtle, marjeram ("rigani"), etc are found in Akamas.

Fauna

Many writers underline the wild life of Akamas in the past, particularly the wild boar. Currently hares, partridges, hedgehogs, foxes, bats and a variety of lizards can be seen. The Mediterranean chameleon can also be spotted. The habitat of Akamas is also ideal for various species of snakes, though only the blunt-nosed viper can be dangerous.

Akamas is the stopover place for the main bird migration route from Europe to Africa and millions of birds, of hundred of species, fly over the area particularly in spring and autumn. A number of colourful butterflies can be seen in many places of Akamas. The griffon vulture which used to live on the cliffs of Akamas and other precipitous slopes does not exist any more.

A number of turtles visit the west coasts of Pafos, finding refuge in sandy beaches where they lay their eggs in August-September. They will lay their eggs in a hole which they dig in the sand. They will bury them until they are naturally incubated in the sand for one and a half months, while the mother turtles return to the sea. For the protection of these turtles a hatchery has been established at Lara(Ammoudi), functioning in the summer months. Besides, each year a number of hatchlings are taken to the sea cages of Pafos harbour to be reared.

Churches and settlements

According to tradition there are as many as 101 churches in the area, with current names as Agioi Fanentes, Panagia Vlou, Osia Maria, Agios Konon, Agios Epifanios, Agios Georgios, Agios Nikolaos, Agia Marina, Agios Mamas, Agia Paraskevi etc. The numerous churches, and the impeccably carved limestone blocks, dispersed in the landscape of Akamas, testify to the existence of a number of very old rural settlements. Most probably the settlements date back to the Roman or Proto-Christian times and were dense during the Byzantine era. Their decline probably coincides with the Arab raids during which the settlements were either totally destroyed or were obliged to move inland where the present settlements of Arodes, Ineia, Drouseia, Androlikou etc lie. It is not surprising that currently no rural settlement is found along the 30 km coastline of the Akamas forest.

According to the University of Aarhus excavations, which have not yet been completed, the landscape of Akamas around Agios Konon with its extensive terracing, seems to have been abandoned around 800 A.D. or even earlier. Most of the

Rocky coastal cliff east of Akamas

buildings were erected during the Early Byzantine period, though ruins dated to the Late Roman period have also been found.

Legends and traditions

The region of Akamas is full of legends and traditions. Karavopetres (ship rocks), lying in the sea west of the old monastery of Panagia Vlou and west north-west of Ineia, are the rocks where, according to tradition, the Saracens, the well-known pirates of the Middle Ages, moored their boats before indulging to looting, burning and destruction of chapels, monasteries and households. The old monastery of Panagia Vlou was destroyed in this manner. According to tradition, Madonna could not stand the contempt of a monastery devoted to her, and immediately transformed the corsairs' boats into rocks, currently petrified in the sea.

Nearly every place-name in Akamas is tied up with a myth or a legend, a number of which most probably originate in the difficult years of the Frankish and Turkish rule of Cyprus.

Almost all isolated rocks, wells and hills in Akamas are associated with a thryll. This is true as far as the Baths of Aphrodite or the Cave of Rigaina or even the Rocks of Digenis are concerned. On the "Vouni tis Rigainas" or the "Hill of Sotira" is the site where Aphrodite or Rigaina used to stand and gaze at the landscape around. The Tower of Rigaina, the place-names Santalies, Stavropigi, Skoteini, Pissouros and Smigies are other places associated with Aphrodite or Rigaina. At Fontana Amorosa, Aphrodite, the Goddess of Love and Beauty, used to take her bath. Afterall, the fruitful Greek imagination chose Cyprus out of all Greek islands as the birthplace of the Goddess of Love and Beauty. This is a symbolical realization of the islands' natural beauties and its romantic, poetic environment.

119

Sand dunes fringing Ammoudi beach

Akamas can be approached through three different directions: (a) via Agios Georgios (Pegeia), along the extreme western, earthen, coastal road, (b) via the Baths of Aphrodite, along the extreme eastern, earthen, coastal road, and (c) via Neo Chorio and Smigies.

A. Following the western coastal road from Agios Georgios (Pegeia)

Followng this route, the visitor encounters a large fine-grained sandy beach, called Toxeftra or Agios Theodoros, east of which a track leads to the mouth of Avakas gorge. The gorge has already been described. *(see Laona-Arodes p.94).* On top of a marine terrace a restaurant has recently been set up, from where an extensive and panoramic view of the area can be obtained. Along the coast the calcarenite rocks, under the influence of sea water, form large and small landforms, including caves, sharp promontories, little bays and many other sculptured phenomena. Flora along the route consists of lentisk, asphodels,

juniper, gorse, thyme and further northwards rockrose, wild carob, olive trees as well as strawberry trees.

The earthen road continues through Agioi Fanentes, where only ruins of the church can be traced, before another noticeable beach, that of Lara, is reached. The beach is surrounded by the same type of vegetation and is fringed by private properties. The sandy beach, under good weather, is recommended for swimming. With its semi-circular shape, it extends to about 1,5 km. A restaurant, south-west of the beach, lying on a terrace, functions during the summer months.

North of the beach on an elevated limestone outcrop, well-known as "Aliki Laras" (salty lake of Lara), sea water has created a number of hollows, caves, sharp surfaces, even holes from where you can look at the sea-water underneath. In the small hollows, salt is formed after the winter sea water is evaporated. In the past, villagers from nearby settlements collected salt from this area. Even the ruined custom house can be seen. Huge blocks of stone, arrayed in a line can be traced in the area. It constituted a fortification wall, dating back to the Mycenean times.

North of the limestone surface, which as it protrudes into the sea appears like a tiny peninsula, lies another beach fringed by sandy dunes, known as **Ammoudi.** It has a horse-shoe shape with two edges ending up in small cliffs. The beach has a length of about 400 m and a width of 30 m. The sand dunes reach a height of about 15m supported by lentisks of an umbrella-shape. Amphorae on the bottom of the sea, south of Ammoudi, most probably testify to the site of an ancient shipwreck. What, however, impresses on the beach is the **Turtle Hatchery,** established in 1978. Turtles coming from the west, arrive at this isolated beach to lay their eggs, mainly in August-September, before they carry on their journey. At the same time turtle eggs from other beaches of Cyprus are carried here to be hatched under safe conditions. The makeshift hatchery functions only during the summer months.

Lara is shown on Mas Latrie's map of 1862, as a tiny settlement. The whole of Lara area was and still is used by the shepherds of the neighbouring villages for transhumance purposes, particularly in winter months. A few sheep and goats are raised all the year round. In the private scattered plots of land the traveller can discern makeshift stone-built dwellings, known as "stiadia", used by farmers in winter time.

Further north of Lara the traveller can see a few huge blocks or rocks in the sea, known as Karavopetres (ship rocks), where, according to tradition, Saracens, the well-known pirates of the Middle Ages, moored their boats before indulging in looting, burning and destruction of chapels, monasteries and households. It is said that in Akamas, in the past, there were as many as 101 churches, some of which can be traced even nowadays.

The old monastery of Vlou (Tyflou=of the Blind), which, according to tradition, has been looted and destroyed by the Saracens, lies east of the main road. Only a modern chapel, on the site of the old monastery, is currently preserved.

Another locality with sculptured caves, appearing as tiny cells on the limestone, known as "Erimites" (Hermit dwellings), most probably has much to say, particularly after some research.

As you follow the route northwards, a number of isles appear on the west, like Geranisos, Kioni, Koppos and Kannoudia. At Geranisos tiny beach, close to a sheepfold, extremely dark basalt pebbles, lying under crystal-clear shallow sea water, are noticeable. North-east of Geranisos isle, on the right hand side of the earthen road, at the locality of Damalospilios, stands a ruined cistern, possibly Byzantine in origin, while close by and for a distance there is a sculptured channel on the limestone outcrop, transporting water from the stream to the cistern. It is another testimony of the organized agricultural activity of Akamas in past centuries. It is advisable to consult local shepherds for the site of the cistern and the old irrigation channel.

The route ends up at Kioni, since from this point the training grounds of the British Forces do not permit further penetration into the Akamas promontory. A black marble column in the sea, is most probably a testimony of some cultural phenomenon, not yet explored. Some people place the outport of ancient Akamantis at this point, where in the summer months a fishing shelter functions. A few kilometres east of Kioni, lies the chapel of Agios Konon where the church and other traces of an ancient settlement abound. Gunnis mentions that below the ruins of Agios Konon lies a Hellenistic-Roman necropolis.

Baths of Aphrodite

Close to Agios Konon, old threshing floors, possibly medieval, as well as a sculptured olive-press on the limestone outcrop can be observed. The unique olive-press, has been protected by an umbrella-shaped lentisk. The local shepherd can show the olive-press to interested visitors.

B. Following the eastern coastal road through the Baths of Aphrodite

At the Baths of Aphrodite the road from Polis and Latsi comes to an end. The tourist pavillion close by, built on a rather steep cliff, serves food, particularly fresh fish, while a number of steps lead the traveller to a very calm sea with crystal clear waters. The pebbled beach and the huge blocks of rocks on the sea bed render the sea ideal for underwater exploration. Though not an extensive sandy beach, quite a few people do swim in the clear waters.

The coastline is rocky with lush vegetation reaching the sea. There are many variations of colour in both the vegetation and the sea water.

A path leads from the pavillion to the **Baths of Aphrodite** amid a dense vegetation. On both sides of the narrow trail lentisks, cypress trees, caper, bramble, wild carob and olive trees, fig trees, eucalyptus and green-yellowish fleabane abound. At the base of the limestone, on the fissures of the rock, grow fig-trees with their broad-leaved branches giving abundant shade. Green mosses colour the rock adding to the beauty of the environment. The water drops from "a thousand silver threads to the pool below". The semi-circular pool has a depth of about half a metre and a perimeter of about five metres. It is not surprising that the fruitful Greek imagination chose this particular place to locate the baths of the Goddess of Love

Staring at the picturesque coastline of Akamas ▶

Quarrying, a few centuries ago, gave rise to the "theatre" in the heart of Akamas

and Beauty. According to tradition, if one bathes in the pool, eternal youth will be bestowed upon him. At least one can wash his hands or his face with the divine waters of Venus. However, it is forbidden to enter the pool for swimming and the water is not drinkable.

From the Baths of Aphrodite a narrow, winding, earthen road-not recommended to everybody unless a special car is used-following the coastline, amid a fascinating and unique in pictures landscape, leads the visitor to the Tower of Rigaina. Whether the Tower of Rigaina (Queen) was a monastery or a manor house has not yet been clarified. I.K. Peristianis mentions the frescoes on the walls which have probably been worn out. Recent archaeological excavations have been carried out and the site is currently protected. It is now believed that the building was probably a monastery. On the right, a few hundred metres, one can look at the tiny isle of St George emerging above sea water. The locality of Agios Nikolaos, south-east of Fontana

Amorosa is an interesting coastal strip of land with broken pottery which probably testifies to an old settlement. Frescoes are still present on the ruined church of Agios Nikolaos, lying next to ponds and ruined buildings. Quarrying is evident on the coastland with a unique landform appearing like an open-air theatre. Quarrying is evident also on the tiny isle of Chamili, close to Fontana Amorosa. **Fontana Amorosa** is a beautiful area and the refuge, in past historical times, of ships which either sought protection in the cove or supply of fresh water. Currently, it is an ideal place for swimming. Tradition has Aphrodite taking her baths in this place.

Ariosto describes the place with some lovely verses: *"Nowhere else in the world have I seen women and virgins so lovely and attractive".*

The water of the well lies a few metres below the surface, though during historical times the table water might have been higher and closer to the surface. If the visitor continues his journey northwards a broken ship will he encountered, stationed for decades in a cove.

C. Following the middle route via Agios Minas to the central areas

West of Neo Chorio is the arched chapel of Agios Minas with some mural paintings and a recently restored fountain. Close by are the foundations of a larger church which most probably served a large crowd of people. The route takes the visitor to Smigies, close to the ruined buildings of a forest station, functioning until a few decades ago. Smigies with its cool water, the wooden tables and seats as well as all other amenities is a picnic site, particularly for summer excursionists. In the location of Santalies, Stavropigi, Skoteini, Pissouros and Smigies, which are all close to each other, the traveller comes across the most wonderful myths concerning Digenis and Rigaina (Queen). At Santalies their little game was interrupted because they lost each other.

Fresco traces in the ruined church of Agios Nikolaos

Suddenly they came across each other at Stavropigi, because of the existence of a spring there. Somewhere else, because of darkness, Digenis could not find the Queen and so the place was called Skoteini (= Dark). On another hill, the Queen surprised Degenis, passing as a shadow next to him but he could not catch her because it was dark (Pissouri). From that time the hill was called Pissouros. Nevertheless they were reunited and embraced at Smigies.

Not far away from Smigies and before one approaches Mavri Shinia, there are the foundations of the church of Agia Paraskevi. In its present condition it has nothing to exhibit, except to confirm the strong tradition that in "the area of Akamas, during the Byzantine era, 101 churches existed, scattered throughout the area".

Following a northern direction one comes across the locality of Magnisia, where in the past magnesia was quarried and exported.

The ruined buildings and all other disused equipment is still there. Close by stands the locality of Kefalovrysia with dense pine-trees. It is worth mentioning that at another locality of Akamas black earth was quarried for export in past decades. However, the travel could end at Vouni tis Sotiras, close to the eastern coastline. The view from Sotira is extensive and unique. Pictures of unconceivable beauty and of rare colours unfold before your eyes. After all you stand between the Baths of Aphrodite and Fontana Amorosa.

SMIGIES PICNIC SITE

It is situated 2 km west of Neo Chorio village and has a capacity of 120 persons. It is equipped with car parking, toilets, piped drinking water, tables and benches, barbecue facilities and children's play areas.

Nature Trails in Akamas

There are four interesting nature trails in Akamas for those who prefer walking.

1. Aphrodite Trail. The trail starts and ends up at the Baths of Aphrodite and passes from the Tower of Rigaina. It is approximately 7,5 km long and the walk time varies from 2 to 4 hours. The section between the Start point and the Tower of Rigaina is shared with the Adonis trail *(see map of Akamas Trails).*

2. Adonis Trail. The trail starts from the Baths of Aphrodite passes from the Tower of Rigaina and ends up at the start point via a southern route. The length of the trail is 7,5 km and the walk time varies from 2 to 4 hours.

3. Smigies Trail. This trail starts from Smigies picnic site and ends up at the starting point. It includes two routes, one of 2,5 km and a longer one of 5 km. The walk time is approximately 1 hour for the first route and 2 hours for the second.

4. Pissouromoutti Trail. This trail starts and ends up at Smigies picnic site via a southern route.Its length is 3 km and walk time is approximately 1,5-2 hours.

Akamas Nature Trails

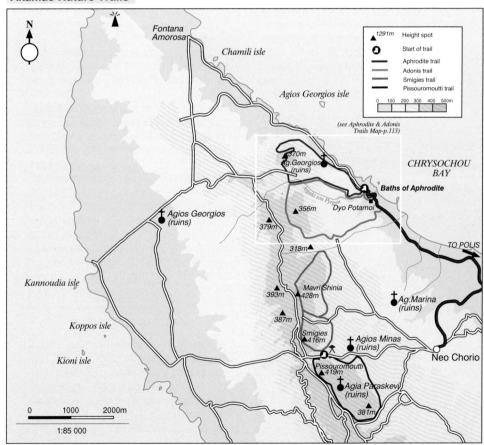

© SELAS LTD

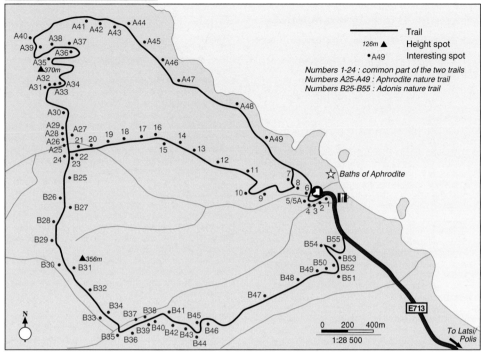

Source: CTO/Dept.of Forests

NUMBERS 1-24: COMMON PART OF APHRODITE & ADONIS TRAIL

1. CAROB TREE *Ceratonia siliqua*. Carob, Olive and Lentisk are important constituents of the maquis. Carob is one of the most characteristic trees of the drier parts of the Eastern Mediterranean region and is most commonly cultivated. The pod, which was locally known as "black gold" due to its contribution to the National Economy (at least in the past) in addition to its other uses, is valuable fodder for animals.

2. OLIVE TREE *Olea europaea*. Olive had its origin in the Orient, yet by the end of the pre-christian era was cultivated throughout the whole Mediterranean region.

3. LENTISK *Pistacia lentiscus*.

4. BRAMBLE *Rubus sanctus*.

5. According to legend, here in the cool, clear pond, the Goddess of Love took her bath.

5A. FIG TREE *Ficus carica*. This is the wild form of the well known cultivated variety.

6. EUCALYPT *Eucalyptus camaldulensis*.

7. SAGE *Salvia fruticosa*. A popular infusion (tea) made from its dried aromatic leaves is believed to have medicinal properties.

8. Cairns are permanent signs to delimit forest land.

9. GOLDEN DROP *Onosma fruticosum*. Endemic; native only to Cyprus.

10. GROMWELL *Lithodora hispidula ssp. versicolor*.

11. HEADED THYME *Thymus capitatus*. It is a typical member of the maquis and garigue. Its aromatic leaves produce an oil which has medicinal properties and is used in perfumery and cosmetics. Honey produced in areas where this shrub is abundant has a characteristic flavour and is highly valued.

12. VIEW POINT.

13. As you walk, notice the hard crust of calcium carbonate which is locally called "Kafkalla": it was formed years ago when calcium carbonate was washed downwards and accumulated in thin layers on top of secondary depositions of calcareous materials.

14. CALABRIAN PINE *Pinus brutia*. Calabrian Pine is the commonest of the conifers on the island and it is in fact the principal forest tree.

15. GREEN BRIER *Smilax aspera*. This woody climber is common in thickets and hedges all over the island.

16. CAROB TREE.

17. LIMESTONES.

18. VIEW POINT.

19. ROCK ROSE *Cistus monspeliensis*. This pretty shrub, which is common elsewhere in the Mediterranean, is found from sea level to about 650m in isolated patches.

20. WICK WEED *Phlomis cypria var. occidentalis*. Endemic.

21. ROYAL OAK *Quercus infectoria ssp.veneris*.

22. The ruins of "Pyrgos tis Rigaenas". The Tower of the Queen.

23. Fountain
24. STORAX *Styrax officinalis.*

APHRODITE NATURE TRAIL CONTINUES FROM A25-A49

A25. OLIVE TREE *Olea europaea ssp. oleaster.* It is the wild form of the known cultivated variety *Olea europaea* met earlier (No.2 on the common part of the trail).
A26. CAROB TREE.
A27. THORNY BROOM *Calycotome villosa.* It grows from sea level to about 1200m. In early spring, in areas where it is abundant, it makes a pretty show with its aromatic yellow flowers.
A28. THORNY GORSE *Genista sphacelata var. sphacelata.*
A29. LENTISK.
A30. STRAWBERRY TREE *Arbutus andrachne.* This beautiful small tree or shrub is quite common and found in areas up to 1300m. Its reddish fruit, reminiscent of strawberries, is edible but not very palatable.
A31. ROCK ROSE *Cistus monspeliensis.*
A32. ROCK ROSE *Cistus parviflorus.* This pretty shrub, occurs only on limestone soils.
A33. ROCK ROSE *Cistus salviifolius.* This shrub is common all over the island up to 1700m. Its leaves, contrary to other species of the genus *Cistus,* are hardly aromatic.
A34. ROCK ROSE *Cistus monspeliensis x parviflorus.* A hybrid resulting from cross-breeding between two different species, that is between *Cistus monspeliensis* and *Cistus parviflorus.*
A35. VIEW POINT.
A36. THORNY BURNET *Sarcopoterium spinosum.* This pioneer species is the commonest of all shrubs in the maquis and garigue in all parts of the island, from sea level up to an altitude of 1250m.
A37. VIEW POINT.
A38. This is the third time you've seen this species so identification should be easy.
A39. The downhill area has been recently cleared by fire.
A40. SAGE.
A41. THORNY GORSE.
A42. PHOENICIAN JUNIPER *Juniperus phoenicea.* This is the most common species in the Akamas region. It grows up to an altitude of 700m. Juniper, in addition to its medicinal uses, is well known for its flavouring and aromatic properties.
A43. GROMWELL.
A44. VIEW POINT.
A45. LENTISK HYBRID *Pistacia x sapportae.* This pretty shrub is a hybrid between Lentisk *Pistacia lentiscus* and Terebinth *Pistacia terebinthus* and it is very rare.
A46. CALABRIAN PINE
A47. STRAWBERRY TREE *Arbutus andrachne.*
A48. VIEW POINT.
A49. VIEW POINT.

ADONIS NATURE TRAIL CONTINUES FROM B25-B55

B25. PHOENICIAN JUNIPER *Juniperus phoenicea.* This is the commonest species in the Akamas region, growing at altitudes as high as 700m.
B26. STRAWBERRY TREE *Arbutus andrachne.* This beautiful small tree or shrub is quite common and found up to 1300m.
B27. Eroded site.
B28. THORNY GORSE *Genista sphacelata var. sphacelata.*

B29. The trail now joins a forest road, constructed by the Forestry Department to serve a forest nursery which has now been abandoned.
B30. As you walk on, notice to your right the thick stand of Calabrian Pine.
B31. Poor quality site due to the existence of moisture, one of the factors controlling tree growth which is here the limiting factor.
B32. HEADED THYME. *Thymus capitatus.*
B33. An abandoned forest nursery.
B34. Potable water.
B35. MYRTLE *Myrtus commumis.* This decorative shrub is common near water sources and in moist places all over the island up to 1700m. As a symbol of love and peace, Myrtle was held sacred and it has been used to decorate the entrance of churches, schools and other public buildings during celebrations.
B36. As you walk along this steep limestone rock, depending of course on the time of year you are visiting the area, notice, at its lower part, different species characteristic of this rocky and rather damp habitat such as Cyclamen *(Cyclamen spp)*, Stonecrop *(Sedum spp)*, Squill *(Scilla cilicica)*, Venus navelwort *(Umbilicus rupestris)*, Fern, Mosses etc.
B37. Notice on your left, along the stream, Cypress *(Cupressus sempervirens).* This plant is very common in Cyprus. Legend says that the island was probably named after it.
B38. TEREBINTH *Pistacia terebinthus.*
B39. ZOULATSIA *Bosea cypria.* This decorative plant, which is endemic, forms an attractive hedge or wall covering.
B40. CHAMAEPEUCE *Ptilostemon chamaepeuce var cyprius.* Endemic.
B41. LENTISK *Pistacia lentiscus.*
B42. VALLOTI *Ballota integrifolia.* Endemic.
B43. CYCLAMEN *Cyclamen persicum.* This is the wild parent of our cultivated winter-flowering cyclamen.
B44. KERMES OAK *Quercus coccifera ssp. calliprinos.* This shrub, which occasionally grows into medium sized trees, is found in middle and lower regions in most parts of the island and exists in a great number of varieties.
B45. Green-brier suppressing both Carob Tree and Aleppo Pine.
B46. This is another example of "Kafkalla". See No.13 (from the common part of the trail).
B47. Samples of maquis.
B48. ROCK ROSE *Cistus monspeliensis.*
B49. ROCK ROSE *Cistus monspeliensis x parviflorus.*
B50. VIEW POINT.
B51. CAIRN.
B52. ALATERNUS *Rhamnus alaternus.*
B53. SMALL-LEAVED MARJIORAN *Origanum majorana var. tenuifolium.* This is endemic and an excellent culinary and medicinal plant. An infusion (tea) made from its dried leaves is regarded as very beneficial in cases of the common cold, tonsilitis and pharyngitis.
B54. SAGE *Salvia fruticosa.*
B55. THORNY BROOM *Calycotome villosa.* This is a typical member of the maquis and garigue, from sea level to about 1200m. In early spring, it makes a pretty show with its aromatic yellow flowers.

Source: CTO/Dept. of Forests.

EXPLORING PAFOS DISTRICT THROUGH THE VALLEYS

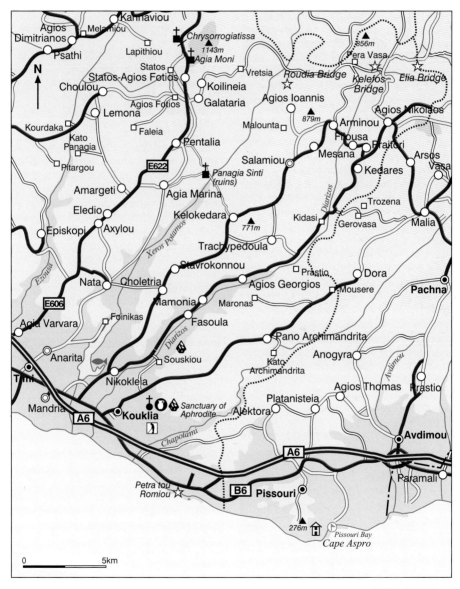

© SELAS LTD

a) Along the Chapotami valley

Route: Archimandrita, Maronas, Mousere

The route from Kouklia to **Archimandrita** is very picturesque, passing through a dissected landscape with a rich natural vegetation. However, if the visit is realised during the autumn months, rare vegatation colours appear before the eyes of the traveller. At Orites there is an experimental station for goats and sheep operating since the 1950's.

The settlement of Kato Archimandrita does not exist any more, as its inhabitants have, since 1964, left the village and moved to Pano Archimandrita.

Archimandrita has a rare place of interest, the Tomb of the 318 Holy Fathers. In a cave, close to the settlement, probably an original Roman tomb, converted later to a chapel and painted, 318 Holy Fathers were buried. Nowadays, the visitor can only see the fresco of Agios Onoufrios. According to tradition, 318 Holy Fathers, persecuted from Syria, arrived at Pissouri and with the company of an archimandrite walked to Archimandrita, through Alektora. At Archimandrita, they were killed by the pagans and their sculls and bones were buried in the cave, known today as the Tomb of the 318 Holy Fathers. On the top of a hill, east of Agios Georgios, lies the isolated and deserted,

Cave of 318 Holy Fathers

since 1975, village of **Maronas**.

Mousere, a medieval settlement, is currently almost deserted. Some parts of cobbled streets witness old road communication links of the village with Pafos and Limassol.

b) Travelling along the Diarizos valley

Route: Nikokleia, Souskiou, Fasoula, Mamonia, Agios Georgios, Trachypedoula, Prastio, Kidasi, Kedares, Filousa, Praitori, Agios Nikolaos, Medieval Bridges, Pera Vasa.

The valley of Diarizos is currently followed by many travellers from Pafos to Platres/Troodos, as it is the shortest and most picturesque route. A techno-economic study has already been prepared and it is anticipated that soon a good road along the valley will be constructed, in order to facilitate quick and comfortable link between Pafos and the summer resorts of Platres/Troodos.

Nikokleia, built on the left bank of Diarizos, and lying close to the Asprokremmos dam, cultivates, as it is obvious, irrigable crops, like citrus, beans and peanuts. A restaurant, housed in a spacious, traditional house, serves the travellers along the Diarizos valley.

Local people recall the functioning of the old water-mill as well as the cultivation of mulberry-tree for the production of silk. The church of Agios Dimitrios, built in 1768, does not host any more the marble column and the capital cited by Gunnis.

The closest significant place of interest is no doubt the Aspokremmos dam, with its height of 80 m and its capacity of 51 million cubic metres of water. The lake, particularly its branches, create a fascinating spectacle, aesthetically attractive to the eye, particularly as it lies amid a dry, rainless landscape.

Souskiou, currently a deserted settlement, lies on the right bank of

Diarizos. The archaeological site and the Chalcolithic findings are of immense significance. In a cemetery, close to the settlement, bottle-shaped tombs hewn from the rock, narrowing towards the top, have been unearthed. Small steatite figurines, several tiny cruciform figures used as pendants, necklaces, stone bowls and composite vases placed as tomb gifts to accompany the dead, were found. A copper spiral discovered at Souskiou, testifies the use of copper at the beginning of the 4th millenium B.C.

Fasoula is situated on the left bank of Diarizos river with its minaret constituting the most conspicuous feature of the settlement.

The most impressive feature in Fasoula's landscape is the surface channel along the river's bed which carries water to southern regions.

Mamonia, a very old settlement, is known for the large chiftlick, of about 385 ha, initially a royal estate during the Lusignan-Venetian period. Later on and more specifically in 1948, it was expropriated from its absentee big landowners, and currently it is distributed to renters.

The village is also known for the Hasamboulia, who terrorized Cyprus in 1890. The criminal activity of the three Turkish brothers around 1894-5, before being arrested by the police, was particularly intense. A water-mill is still preserved in te village, next to a traditional restaurant on the main road.

Agios Georgios. Greenery in Agios Georgios is abundant, while tall alder and plane trees as well as some poplar trees raise their height above the normal size of fruit trees. Obviously the village, prior to 1571, was Greek, as testified by its name and the ruined church of Agios Georgios.

On a gentle slope, facing the valley of Diarizos, lies **Trachypedoula,** which most probably owes its name to the rough and infertile landscape with the rocks of the Mamonia Complex pojecting above the ground.

Trachypedoula is rich in traditional architecture with stone-built two-storeyed houses, tall walls around the dwelling, with some oxen still used for the cultivation of the slopy lands. The rural character of the settlement is almost intact.

East of Trachypedoula, on the road Trachypedoula-Kidasi, stands a most spectacular rock outcrop, which is currently the subject of preservation in the area. The travellers, as they traverse the Diarizos valley, pass through the rock.

Prastio, a Turkish Cypriot settlement, is abandoned since 1964. The church of Archangelos Gavriil, a building of the 15th century, is currently deserted, while on a projecting rock outcrop, close to the main road, stands the church of Profitis Ilias. However, the historic monastery of Agios Savvas of Karonos, on the right side of Diarizos valley, is currently deserted. According to Tsiknopoullos, the church was originally arched and three-aisled. The monastery was most probably set up in 1120 but was burned in 1467. An iscription over the west door informs us that the church was rebuilt in 1501 and restored in 1724. The monastery of Agios Savvas owned two annexes, one at Trachypedoula and another at Pano Arodes.

Kidasi is currently inhabited by two refugee families. The original site of the settlement was a few kilometres north of the present site, close to the bed of the river. It was hit by the earthquakes of 1953, a factor that necessitated its removal. An old water-mill, a few centuries-old oak-trees and a natural spring by the main road are the remnants of the previous settlement. A coffee-shop has been established under the oak-tree which attracts passers-by during the summer months.

Kedares is a vine-producing village known for its zivania (local alcohol drink)

Kelefos bridge

and its wine. Most of the houses, are built in traditional architecture.

P.Dikaios, identified traces of neolithic settlement. The village was initially built at a different site but, on account of a disease, probably in the 18th century, most of the inhabitants died. Those who survived, built a new village at the present locality of the settlement. What survived from the old settlement is the place-name "Palio Chorio" (old village) as well as the original spring. Most probably the present restored church of Agios Antonios, next to the main road, belonged to the old settlement.

However, I. Tsiknopoullos cites that Agios Antonios was the church of a disbanded monastery, dating back to the 17th century. He also mentions the portable icons of the church, of the 17th and 18th centuries, which for safety reasons are now kept in the new parish church of Kedares.

Filousa, like the neighbouring settlements is a wine-producing village. West of Filousa the broad bed of Diarizos permits the exploration of the valley which is rich in tall plane and pine-trees as well as tamerisk. The tunnel that diverts the waters of Diarizos to Kouris starts from the administrative boundaries of Filousa.

In the village there are two ancient churches: The church of Agios Nikolaos, steep-pitched and single-aisled, at a amall distance from the village, was originally a monastery. The large icon of St Nikolaos, dated 1520, was initially transferred to the parish church and later to the Byzantine Museum of Pafos. The church of Agia Marina is steep-pitched with a low belfry tower.

Praitori, close to the district boundaries of Pafos and Limassol, depends entirely on the monoculture of vines, particularly of the black variety.

Despite depopulation, the few inhabitants continue to prepare zivania (local alcohol) and wine. Praitori was a royal estate during the Frankish period, though whether its name is from the Latin word "praetor", and therefore Roman, is not yet proved. The church of Panagia Chryseleousa is a modern building constructed on the foundations of an ancient church which was destroyed by fire. The 16th century icon of Panagia, now silver-covered, was saved by a Turk who rushed through the flames and bore it to safety.

The Turkish-Cypriot village of **Agios Nikolaos** is most probably a Byzantine settlement, while during the Frankish period it was a royal estate. The interesting church of Archangelos Michail was converted into a mosque after the 1571 conquest of Cyprus by the Turks. It was orginally a double church serving both Orthodox and Latins. The Latin half was pulled down, though its foundations still exist. In the Orthodox part there remains a vast 16th century painting of Archangelos Michail on the north wall while some portable icons are currently kept in the Byzantine Museum of Pafos. A large slab of marble lies in the apse, a Byzantine work of the 13th century. A portion of the preserved iconostasis belongs to the 16th century.

Agios Nikolaos is a fruit producing village with four refrigerated chambers functioning for the storing of fresh fruit, mainly apples and pears. Within the settlement the minaret with its height dominates the landscape, while along the main road to Troodos and Platres, tavernas, restaurants and coffee-shops have been set up to serve particularly visitors who travel along the Diarizos valley.

Agios Nikolaos, Pafos

Medieval Bridges. In the upper portion of the valleys of Diarizos and Xeros, lie three renowned medieval bridges: *Elia, Kelefos and Roudia.*

Elia, lies west of Foini, amid rich natural vegetation. It is constructed on a tributary of Diarizos. Its width is 2,40 m and its arch 5,50 m. It can be visited easily from an earthen road close by. Following the earthen road towards Pera Vasa, at the locality Platys, lies *Kelefos,* the second medieval bridge. Its width is 2,50 m while its arch is 10,70 m. Water flows all the year round while the natural vegetation is very dense. Alder and plane trees are very tall. It is worth while taking a rest by the bridge, listening to the sweet nightingale and the murmuring of the flowing water, while enjoying the cool breeze, particularly in the summer months.

West of Pera Vasa, on the Xeros river lies *Roudia,* the third bridge. The earthen road leading to Roudia is narrow, winding and isolated. Game is plentiful especially partridges, rock doves as well as wood pigeons. The Roudia bridge, under the shadow of gigantic forest trees, is 2,80 m wide while its arch is 10 m. It was restored in 1975-76. The three bridges, belong to the 16th or 17th century. All of them were constructed to facilitate communication among the various regions of Cyprus. They were used by animal-driven carts, since cars made their appearance only at the beginning of the twentieth century.

The visitor to the medieval bridges of Pafos, inevitably passes through **Pera Vasa,** a deserted settlement, where the largest pine tree of Cyprus was found. The perimeter of the trunk was about 7 metres and its height about 40 metres. The pine-tree, 400 years old, has ceased to exist since 1997 on account of biological maturity.

c) Exploring the settlements on the ridge between Xeros and Diarizos valleys.

> **Route: Choletria, Stavrokonnou, Kelokedara, Salamiou, Malounta, Agios Ioannis, Mesana, Arminou**

Choletria, on the ridge between Xeros and Diarizos, is a new settlement, removed to its present position in 1974, on account of landslides. The old settlement, on a slope facing Xeros river, is now deserted and uninhabited.

On the right bank of the Xeros river, a water-mill still stands in relatively good condition. To the south and towards the old Choletria settlement, near the Xeros river bed, is the church of Agios Panteleimonas; further on, on a small height, next to the river bed is the Ortos area, where archaeological excavations are being carried out. It is still not clear what will emerge, even though at the other side of Choletria, next to Diarizos river bed, the archaeological settlement of Souskiou yielded some remarkable findings. So far the unearthed findings (1993) point out that Ortos was a large settlement, the greatest part of which was eroded away or destroyed by cultivations. It is an aceramic Neolithic settlement where thousands of man-made stone objects were found. Most probably it dates back to 5.400-4.200 B.C.

Stavrokonnou. As a mixed Turkish-Cypriot village it experienced significant increase in population, especially before 1974, when the Turkish-Cypriot leadership gathered Turkish-Cypriots in enclaves. Later, with the 1974 invasion, the inhabitants were transferred to the occupied area of the island. The village retains a mosque, without a minaret, and uses a still to produce zivania.

Kelokedara, a village on the crest between Xeros and Diarizos, south-west of Salamiou, is no longer the administrative centre with manifold services, as it was in the past. In the last century the village history was associated with notorious robbers and criminals from Mamonia village, who were known as "Hasamboulia". The three Turkish-Cypriot fugitives and robbers lived in the area, particularly in Kelokedara, hiding themselves from people. Their nickname came from the first of the fugitives, Hasan Achmet Poulli. The whole story started in 1887 and ended nine years later with their execution.

Salamiou, built on the ridge of the two valleys, enjoys a vast view towards many directions. A strong tradition is preserved in the village, according to which, while St Paul and St Barnabas were journeying from Salamis to Pafos, in the first century A.D., they rested here in the middle of the day and took a meal. The olive stones which they threw away grew and became olive trees, now very old with thick trunks, are known as "Apostolic olive trees".

Even the churches of the village are loaded with history. The large parish church of Agia Varvara, with its marble iconostasis was built with donations and free voluntary work on behalf of the villagers themselves. The old church of Agios Georgios is restored and protected. The church of Panagia (Madonna) Eleousa, previously a monastery, was built in 1550 and repaired in 1916. The icon of Panagia Eleousa is of the 16th century, while others belong to the 17th century. According to Kyprianos, the monastery of Eleousa was functioning during the Turkish period. Round the present church grow some oak-trees, which are said to be sacred to the Virgin and must not be cut.

To the south-west of Agios Ioannis and near Xeros river a number of deserted and ruined constructions testify the existence of the settlement of **Malounta,** which was abandoned in 1953 due to earthquakes.

Agios Ioannis, a Turkish-Cypriot settlement, is basically a wine-producing village, even though it has areas of land where fruit trees, almond, olive trees and vegetables are cultivated.

The architecture of the houses with the elongated rooms, the two-storeyed houses built with hewn limestone blocks, are no different from the architecture of other buildings which one comes across in the Limassol and Pafos vine villages. Travelling along Agios Ioannis area and Xeros valley during the autumn months, you will often come across a few vultures with quite a few crows flying alongside or sitting on their wings without any fear or danger whatsoever. These vultures which hunt carcasses do not seem to be interested in live birds. A vulture restaurant is planned to be established at Agios Ioannis where a few vultures, still alive in Cyprus, will find a regular meal.

The houses in **Mesana** are built in the traditional architecture of vine-growing villages with stills in almost all house-yards for the production of zivania (local alcohol drink) and wine.

On the bank of the river, about 3 km from the village, is the Monastery of Agios Georgios Komanon, built in the 15th century. The cells do not exist any more, while the arched church preserves some paintings. On the north wall is the large

Old water-mill, Choletria

Apostolic olive trees, believed to date back to the times of St Paul, Salamiou

Monastery of Agios Georgios Komanon, Mesana

mural painting of St George with scenes from his martyrdom, while opposite on the lower section is the painting of Archangelos Michail. Among those who visited the monastery in the past, is the Russian monk Barsky in 1735, who wrote that the monastery had a beautiful tiled church but the cells were ruined.

Arminou is primarily a grape-producing village. In the past many public services focused in the village settlement served the neighbouring villages. It is not known whether in the past the settlement was inhabited by Armenians, nor is it clear whether the name of the settlement has any relation to the Armenians. The church of the Holy Cross was built in the middle of the eighteenth century. Its chief treasure is a gilted wooden cross, subsequently taken to the new parish church of Agia Marina. It is said that the cross was kept at Souskiou, but came to Arminou of its own volition many years ago. The present church has an old iconostasis and an old praying stand, while the portable icons are relatively modern. Barsky, the Russian monk who visited Arminou in 1735 writes that in the monastery of the Holy Cross there were a few cells.

d) Exploring the settlements on the ridge between Xeros and Ezousa valleys

> **Route: Anarita, Foinikas, Nata, Axylou, Eledio, Amargeti, Agia Marina, Pentalia, Galataria, Faleia, Koilineia, Vretsia**

About 2 km north-east of Timi lies the village of **Anarita,** engaged in farming and animal raising.

Not far from the village lies the ruined Byzantine monastery of Agios Onisiforos, who was born in Constantinople and later became an admiral in the service of the Byzantine Empire. He took part in many battles but finally gave up all positions and power and settled in Anarita as a humble hermit. After his death he was declared a saint, while the place he lived was replaced by a monastery.

The parish church of Agia Marina stands in the middle of the settlement where the modern church of Agios Epifanios lies too. Not far from the settlement there is a well, plastered inside, and surrounded by paved pebbles from the beach indicating most probably Venetian origin.

Foinikas, on the left bank of Xeropotamos, has now been deserted. The large Asprokremmos dam, which was constructed on the Xeropotamos river, next to Foinikas, with a capacity of 51.000.000 c.m., covered a section of the village.

Foinikas belonged to the Small Commandaria, which included another four villages. In particular Small Commandaria was connected with Foinikas and Anogyra villages.

Nata, on the west slope of Xeropotamos, is a somewhat isolated village, which was struck by earthquakes in 1953.

Nata is rich in traditional architecture with spacious courtyards, large wine jars and two-storeyd houses. In one case a road passes under a vaulted construction.

The church of Panagia Eleousa, now in

ruins, with its thick walls and traces of frescoes, found on the earthen road towards Agia Marina, is worth visiting. It is a relatively large church, possibly of the Frankish era, testifying that the population in those days was large.

Axylou. The initial site of the village, north-west of today's position and nearer to Ezousa Valley, was found to be unsuitable, particularly after the catastrophic earthquakes of 1953. Thus, a year later, the settlement was removed to the crest of the ridge between the Ezousa and Xeros rivers. Only ruins of the old settlement remain, some centuries-old olive trees, and the church site. The site of the old church of Agios Alexandros is well known and the refugees, established in the village after 1974, light candles there, even though it is now a cultivated vineyard. According to Leontios Machairas, three Alaman Saints came and settled in the village: "Agios Alexandros, Agios Charetis and one Epifanios".

The old ruined settlement of **Eledio,** is near the north-west of the new settlement. What is preserved, is the old spring of the village, the half-ruined church of Agia Eirini, and some centuries-old olive trees. The inhabitants can recall that around the church of Agia Eirini there was an annex with a monk. Nevertheless, the sources are not clear, as to the existene of either a monastery or an annex in the village.

The decision to abandon the original settlement was made after the catastrophic earthquakes of 1953, even though the removal to the new settlement, on the main arterial road, was not achieved until 1955.

Amargeti. The village no longer relies exclusively on vines and grain. Drilling and natural springs have allowed the village to cultivate citrus, fruit trees and vegetables.

Tourist apartments and country homes have recently started to appear, while the

Holy doors from the church of the Holy Cross, Arminou, 18th c.A.D.

earthen road which connects Amargeti with Lemona has been partly asphalted and is used by hikers from the Pafos tourist area.

Amargeti is known for the archaeological site of Petros Anthropos, even though a visitor will not come across any excavations or the real site. Inscriptions on the base of statues which were found in the area indicate that Apollo Malanthios was worshipped in the area. The inscriptions, which are dedicated to Apollo Malanthios, date from various eras up to the 3rd century B.C. and belong to the Hellenistic and Roman eras. Sakellarios (1890) mentions that "near Amargeti a lot of earthenware pots were found similar to those found in the Mycenae".

Agia Marina is a small, picturesque village with an attractive landscape and pine-covered slopes and ravines, lying north-east of Amargeti, on the left side of Xeropotamos. The beautiful small houses, built with hewn limestone blocks have recently been whitewashed, to the extent that architecture has been violated. Even the church of Agia Marina, which probably dates to previous centuries, has been restored and no longer retains its historical character.

In **Pentalia** there is a remarkable cultural monument, the monastery of Sinti, on the west bank of Xeros river. It is not well known when the monument was built, though its church belongs to the first half of the 16th century. In recent years it was an annex of Kykko monastery. In 1735 the monastery was visited by Barsky, the well-known Russian monk, who described the monastery in great detail. He notes that the monastery depends on Kykko, from where monks and stewards were sent. The monastery has two mills and a few deciduous trees. He describes the monastery as very old, square-shaped, with a big courtyard and a well in the middle. He praises the church with its dome and observes that it was built with great dexterity. Today the monastery is in ruins. However, the well in the middle of the courtyard, and the church with cracks on its walls, are still in existence. The east wing of the monastey, and the north wing, look as if they are two-storeyed buildings in comparison with the west wing which consists of ground floor rooms which were used as stables and barns.

The single-aisled church with its eight-sided dome possibly belongs to the 16th century. It is worth mentioning, as Loizos Philippou refers, that not only Sinti, but Pentalia itself, were annexes of Kykko during 1774, when the Land Registry Code of The Holy Monastery of Kykko was being drafted.

What is remarkable is the fact that two abbots from Kykko monastery came from Pentalia, namely Iosif, and Neofytos. It was Iosif who, with the beginning of the Greek Revolution and when the island's inhabitants were ordered to disarm themselves, ordered all valuable items of the monastery to be placed in a special hiding place. Nevertheless, in 1821 Kutchuk Mehmet ordered the hanging of abbot Iosif. Neofytos, a scholar, also from Pentalia, succeeded abbot Sofronios of Kykko in 1826. Neofytos was the nephew of Iosif, the martyr. Neofytos visited Constantinople and through the Patriarch made every attempt to secure financial support for the monastery which was in danger of collapsing.

Restoration works were initiated in 1994 and by 1998 the monastery with its significant historic and archaeological value was fully restored. In fact it was during the year of the successful restoration that the diploma of Europa Nostra was awarded to the monastery.

In **Galataria,** the visitor can come across three significant places of interest. Firstly, there is the large spring in the "Vlea" area, where the water ends up in an enormous reservoir, from which a relatively large area is irrigated. Secondly, worth visiting is the church of Panagia Galatousa. The original church, according to Gunnis was a 1768 construction with a sun-dial on the north side of the wall. It had some old icons which Greeks and Turks would worship because they believed in her miracles. The church was demolished and very close by a new one was built, also dedicated to Panagia Galatousa. Thirdly, the visitor can visit another small arched church, dedicated to Agios Nikolaos, built on a rock, not very far from Xeropotamos. This little church was built in 1550 and still maintains some frescoes, even though the interior of the church has been blackened by smoke from fires lit by shepherds. There is a tradition regarding the icon and the church of Agios Nikolaos. Not only the Greek-Cypriots but also the Turkish-Cypriots in the area,

Monastery of Sinti, Pentalia

believed that if their animals were sick, they should cut off hairs from their tails and hang them on the church door. They should smear the wound with olive from the candle and if possible, should lead the animals round the church three times.

There is also a tradition that when Digenis was in Vretsia hunting Rigaina (Queen), he threw a rock at her, which fell in Galataria at a spot where two hares were playing. The rock fell in the middle and separated the hares. Since then the area is called "Petra ton Laouthkion" (Rock of the hares).

South of Statos-Agios Fotios lies the deserted Turkish-Cypriot village of **Faleia. Koilineia** is a village whose population is on the decline. There are still a few donkeys, useful in the dissected landscape of Koilineia. Some traditional houses, built with hewn limestone blocks, retain roofs with clay obtained from the "Teratsies" area.

Perhaps the best route to visit the deserted village of **Vretsia** is via Agios Nikolaos-Kelefos bridge-Pera Vasa-Roudia bridge. It is a unique and unforgettable route, though the absence of adequate singposts might be a problem. There is, however a shorter road through Koilineia. Vretsia is a mountainous village with its administrative area including part of the Pafos forest.

Vretsia appears on Venetian maps and according to Florio Bustron it was a Frankish feud. Until recently one could trace the foundations of the church, constructed before Cyprus was conquered by the Turks in 1571.

e) Travelling along the Ezousa Valley

Route: Pitargou, Kato Panagia, Kourdaka, Choulou, Lemona

The Turkish-Cypriot village of **Pitargou**, east of Kallepeia, is now abandoned. The name of the village, before the Turks settled in 1571, was probably Epidavria or

Epidavrion, and it was possibly built by Greeks from Peloponnesus. It was renamed Epidaurum by the Romans, Pithavrio by the Franks and Pithariou/Pittargou during Turkish rule. Mas Latrie refers to Pithavrio and lists it as a feud during the Frankish rule.

Kato Panagia, is currently a place-name inter-related to Pano Panagia. Kato Panagia is used in the winter months by Panagia farmers for animal grazing. According to Loizos Philippou, when the Land Registry Code was prepared for the Holy Monastery of Kykko, it appeared that Kato Panagia was an annex of Kykko in 1774 The Turkish-Cypriot village of **Kourdaka,** to the left of the Letymvou-Choulou road, is currently abandoned.

Kourdaka is mentioned by Machairas, who notes that two saints, Pygon and Christoforos, led a hermit's life in the village.

Choulou is a village with many churches, varied scenery and a variety of products.

The tall minaret which dominates the village, constitutes irrefutable evidence that this was once a mixed Turkish-Cypriot settlement.

The church of Agios Georgios, now restored, about two kilometres west of the village, is single-aisled with a dome and narthex, added later. Initially the entire church was full of frescoes but only a few have survived. The church of Agios Georgios is of the Middle Byzantine era.

The church of Agios Theodoros lies within the settlement. It is now in ruins and could possibly date back to the middle of the 12th century. The parish church of Panagia Pantanassa belongs to the 16th century. It is single-aisled, arched and initially frescoed. The fresco of the Virgin Mary is preserved, albeit blackened by smoke.

In Choulou and Lemona the song of Arodafnousa, in another version, has survived, which tells the story of the love of the feudal lord of Choulou, Moundolif,

Old-style harvesting, still prevalent in a few villages of Pafos

The church of Agios Georgios, Choulou

for the "Rigaina" (Queen) of Lemona. It is not clear whether Hogarth had this love in mind when he wrote about Choulou that it is a "large and rascally village".

Lemona lies south of Choulou and east of Ezousa. In the past Lemona was famous for its silk, and even to this day quite a few mulberry trees are still to be seen. A little distance from the village are olive trees which, according to tradition, belong to Archangelos Michail and nobody may cut them or harm them.

The tale of Arodafnousa is well known to the inhabitants. In fact an elderly woman can recite verses from the poem's version. The feudal lord of Choulou and the noble lady of Lemona fell in love and their secret love was sung by the inhabitants as an idyl between the Rigas (king) and the Rigaina (queen). Today a place-name with the name of Arodafnousa is preserved within the administrative boundaries of the village.

Route: Melamiou, Kannaviou, Agyia

The small Greek-Cypriot settlement of **Melamiou,** south-west of Kannaviou, no longer exists.

Kannaviou. The village at the southern foot of the Pafos forest is on the banks of the Ezousa river. Perhaps it is here, on the banks of Ezousa river, that during the Lusignan and Venetian periods hemp was cultivated, from which the village got its name.

The quiet farming life of the village, the coolness and the greenery, especially during the summer months enchant the visitor. The abundant trees and the summer breeze led to the establishment of more coffee shops and recreation centres in the settlement than a small village would normally maintain. Recently tourist apartments have been built and they are rented to summer holiday makers.

The picnic site of **Agyia,** south of Stavros tis Psokas, in the Pafos forest, is best approached from Kannaviou. To the left of the Kannaviou-Panagia road, where the bridge crosses Ezousa river, there is an asphalted road for about two kilometres and then another earthen road leading to Agyia. The route through the narrow, deep valley of Ezousa, is pleasant and comfortable although in some places the road is narrow. Tall plane and alder trees are found in the river bed and ivy embraces the tree trunks. On the slopes, which are sometimes steep, grow pine trees together with other low bushes. As the relief rises the golden oak makes its appearance together with terebinth, while cicada keeps company to the visitor.

The Agyia picnic site, which can accommodate 200 people, provides benches, a playing area for children, drinkable water, equipment for barbecue and other basic facilities. Most probably this route can be combined with the route Psathi, Agios Dimitrianos, Lapithiou.

Route: Psathi, Agios Dimitrianos, Lapithiou

Psathi lies on a ridge between Polemi and Kannaviou. It enjoys an extensive view towards many directions.

Agios Dimitrianos, east of Psathi, lying on a ridge, is rich in traditional rural architecture.

Lapithiou, a Turkish-Cypriot settlement to the south-west of Chrysorrogiatissa monastery, is now abandoned.

AGYIA PICNIC SITE

It is situated about 11 km north of Kannaviou village, on the right hand side of the road. It has a capacity of about 200 persons. It is equipped with car parking, toilets, piped drinking water, tables and benches, barbecue facilities and children's play areas.

Dense forest vegetation on the way from Kannaviou to Agyia

HILLY VILLAGES OF PAFOS DISTRICT

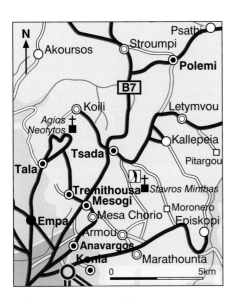

Stavros Minthas monastery

a) Large vine-growing villages

Route: Tsada, Stavros Minthas Monastery, Koili, Kallepeia, Letymvou, Polemi, Stroumpi

Tsada is situated on an undulating chalky landscape, enjoying a limitless view, particularly to the west. Its economy depends on the monoculture of vines. Furthermore, tourist villages and isolated villas are currently being built in the village. Hogarth notes that at Tsada some ancient Roman tombs were unearthed, though systematic archaeological excavations have, not so far been undertaken. Limonidas manuscript refers to the monastery of Minthas which most probably pre-existed the settlement of Tsada. This leads to the possible conclusion that Tsada is a subsequent settlement.

It is not known when **the monastery of Stavros Minthas,** 3 km east of Tsada,

was built, though Tsiknopoullos refers to 1520. Most probably its name is from the plant "mentha". Barsky, the Russian monk who visited the monastery in 1735, writes: "The monastery is dedicated to the Holy Cross. There is only a church, one cell, one monk and one lay brother. The church has a nice architecture. There is a cross much venerated by locals. It was found in the bushes close by". The present church was erected in the year 1740 A.D. by Joachim, bishop of Pafos.

Kyriazis notes that during the first half of the 19th century the Minthas monastery was the seat of Pafos bishopric. The two-storeyed monastery, is currently administered by a monk. The doorway shows Gothic influence, while the south doorway appears to be the work of the 16th century. The iconostasis belongs to the 18th century.

In an area belonging to the monastery a large golf course has recently been established along with a clubhouse.

Koili, north-west of Tsada, fascinates the visitor with its location on a hill with extensive view towards many directions. A few water-mills, now out of use, lie on the bed of Mavrokolympos river. The Telecommunications station is quite tall and visible from long distances.

A few people started building countryside houses on the hill enjoying the abundant and unique view. A tourist village, at the locality *Zelemenos,* has been built, comprising luxurious villas with flowered gardens, mostly bought by wealthy foreigners.

Kallepeia. The settlement is currently spreading along the Tsada-Kallepeia road, a factor that constitutes a threat to its cohesion. The modern church of Agios Georgios is imposing, though the old church is now disused. This church is a long building of unusual shape and thick walls. A stone statue that existed in the church has now disappeared. The neighbouring "monastery" stands on a hill dominating the village. It is built with

local marble while traces of frescoes appear on its walls.

Letymvou is a village of churches. Hogarth, in 1889, enumerated twelve, including the painted church of saints Kyrikos and Ioulitti which impressed him considerably, mainly because of the richness of frescoes, the beauty of persons' expression and the freedom of movement. Until recently a quarry was functioning, producing marble slabs for the floor of traditional houses. The Heroes Monument, the restored fountain, and the oil press in the village square give a distinct colour to the settlement.

What, however, impresses the visitors is the church of Sts Kyrikos and Ioulitti. It is a cruciform in style church with dome, constructed in the 15th century. Marble is plethoric inside, while the exterior walls are built with calcarenite. The interior of the church was entirely covered with paintings, with the exception of the dome. Some preserved paintings are the Birth of Virgin Mary, the Prayer of Anna, the

A villager of Polemi, returning to the village from his field

Wine and grape festival, Stroumpi

Nativity, Baptism, the Rising of Lazarus, the Judgement, the Twelve Apostles and some others. Four other chapels, now ruined, are found around the settlement.

Almost every square metre of the administrative area of **Polemi** is planted with vines. Even a small winery functions in the village, now managed by a big Cypriot wine company.

In the locality Kampos tis Rigainas (Plain of the Queen), on a rise, there is a landform resembling a human seat. On it, according to tradition, Digenis was seated, gazing at the gulf of Chrysochou, ready to attack and kill the Saracens, the well-known pirates, who used to loot and ruin the houses and properties of the Cypriots in the Byzantine times. The exact locality is known as the "Seat of Digenis", while the area is full of Byzantine legends. Besides, the name of the village has a

Byzantine origin.

The church of Panagia Chryseleousa, possibly of the 13th or 14th century, within the built-up area of the village is a noteworthy monument. It is domed, cruciform in style and possibly originally painted. A narthex was added later while a new modern church has been added to the Byzantine building, separated by arches. The narthex was added in 1723, while the iconostasis dates back to the 16th century. Some icons belong to the 17th century and, as Gunnis writes, they are influenced by the Italian Renaissance. Most probably the modern church was added in 1737.

Polemi has many churches, one of which, Agios Georgios, is closely associated with the village of Agios Georgios Silikou, in the Limassol district. According to tradition, the ruined church of Agios

Georgios is the last remnant of a village that disappeared, as its inhabitants left Polemi and built Agios Georgios Silikou, in Limassol.

Hogarth suggests that Polemi dates back to the Roman times.

Stroumpi, a significant communications junction, particularly between Pafos and Polis, is an old settlement. At the locality "Kampos", antiquities unearthed, testify to the ancient origin of the settlement. In Frankish times it was a feud. The original settlement, currently known as Upper Stroumpi (Pano Stoumpi), preserves some traditional houses worth visiting. There were also two wineries as well as a corn-mill. After the catastrophic earthquakes of 1953 the settlement was removed to present-day Stroumpi, often known as Kato Stroumpi (Lower Stroumpi). The new planned settlement, with wide roads is surrounded by flower and fruit gardens, while in the middle stands the church of the Holy Spirit. A recently-built restaurant-taverna functions at the entrance to the village from Pafos. A wine and grape festival called "Dionysia" takes place annually, attracting people from the towns as well as from the neighbouring villages.

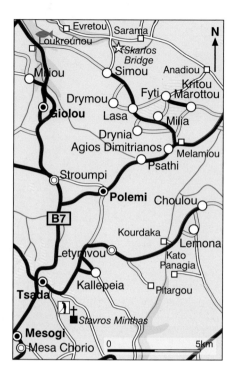

b) Hilly villages west of Pafos Forest

Route: Simou, Drymou, Lasa, Drynia, Milia, Fyti, Kritou Marottou, Anadiou

Simou, east of Chrysochou valley, is rich in natural and cultural characteristics.

Centuries-old terebinths, olive trees and oak-trees, are scattered in the administrative area of the village. The centuries-old terebinth in the middle of the settlement is, according to tradition, as old as the village itself. Traditional architecture is rich. A well, from which water was obtained, before houses were furnished with piped water, still exists in the village. The most important feature of the village, however, is the bridge of Skarfos, dating back to 1618, with a width of 2,75 m and a length of 8,50 m, built

---

AVAILABLE IN POLEMI

Bank

Co-operative Credit Society

Improvement Board

Petrol station

Restaurant

Secondary school

Stadium

Skarfos bridge, Simou

with hewn limestone blocks and pebbles from the river bed.

Drymou, a hilly village between Simou and Lasa, has grown, according to the inhabitants, in seven heighbourhoods. Hogard refers to the marble bowl at Drynia which, he thinks, belongs to Drymou.

At the entrance to the village a carved tomb is preserved, which most probably belongs to the Hellenistic-Roman period. The traditional architecture is very rich with arched rooms, two-storeyed buildings and the abundant use of hewn limestone blocks in the building of houses.

Lasa, between Drymou and Fyti, is being depopulated, despite its rich and impressive traditional architecture. The visitor might even see today the threshing of wheat and legumes still functioning in the threshing-floor of the village, a feature dating back to Homeric times.

Weaving is well-developed in the village, though currently only a few women continue this handicraft. Many houses continue to keep the looms which some members of the family were handling in the last century or even recently. Even carpenters and masons still exercise the art of working the wood and stone, for chair-making as well as for other artifacts.

The traditional architecture at **Drynia** is very rich, while the use of hewn limestone blocks is plethoric. Built with impeccable limestone blocks is the church of Agios Georgios, a building of 1755. The marble bowl, close to the church, belongs, according to Hogarth, to the neighbouring village of Drymou.

Olive mill, Drymou

Table cloth made by Fyti weavers

Milia, beween Fyti and Drynia, is a declining village with about a dozen permanent inhabitants.

Fyti, lying close to the Forest of Pafos and the valley of Stavros tis Psokas, enjoys a vast view towards many directions. In the locality "Akrikous" a centuries-old oak-tree stands next to an old spring of the settlement. Most probably this is the largest oak-tree in Cyprus, with a trunk perimeter of 10 m, a height of 20 m and a cavity in the trunk large enough to accommodate 5-6 persons. In past decades it was used as a stable for oxen or as pen of sheep.

It is, however, the traditional architecture, particularly the well-carved limestone blocks used for the building of elongated rooms, two-storeyed houses or arched double-rooms that fascinate the visitor. Nowhere else in Pafos will the traveller meet this splendid architecture, the product of Fyti's traditional builders. Weaving, is , however, a speciality of Fyti and nobody knows the roots of the handicraft, which are lost in time. In past decades nearly every household kept a "voufa", (loom), while until 30 years ago there were as many as 40 weavers. Currently there are only a few. The designs of Fyti's woven products are plenty and are characterised by their special technique and their aesthetic values. Vivid colours, like the red, the green, the yellow and the blue render them unique. Women at Fyti weave curtains, handkerchiefs, pillow-cases, bed covers, napkins, table-cloths and a number of other products. The visitor can always find a souvenir to buy.

Kritou Marottou, east of Fyti, is a very old village. A part of Pafos forest falls within the administrative bounadries of the village. In the centre of the village, on a slope close to the old church of Agia Marina, the "Octagon" has been built, an impressive building, functioning as a coffee-shop with flowers and grass around.

North of Kritou Marottou lies the abandoned settlement of **Anadiou.** The abandoned houses are not conventional, but special buildings to resist earthquake tremors.

MOUNTAINOUS AND SEMI-MOUNTAINOUS VILLAGES OF PAFOS DISTRICT

a) Semi-mountainous villages

Route: Asprogia, Mamountali, Panagia, Chrysorrogiatissa Monastery Agia Moni Monastery, Statos-Agios Fotios (Ampelitis), Statos, Agios Fotios

Asprogia, west of Panagia, is probably a very old settlement, since, as Hill cites, here iron pyrites was extracted in antiquity.

The presence of a mosque with a small minaret testifies the presence of a few Turkish Cypriots who have recently abandoned the settlement. The steep-pitched church of Agios Epifanios dates back to 1723.

Mamountali is an abandoned settlement south of Asprogia.

Panagia, can be approached either from Pafos or through the mountains of Troodos, via the Cedar Valley or Agios Georgios Emnon. The village has a number of sites worth visiting. The Historic Cultural Centre of Makarios III is open daily except on Mondays. In it are displayed personal belongings of Makarios, particularly photographs concerning his manifold activities. As it is well known, Panagia is the birthplace of Makarios, late Archbishop and president of Cyprus.

Not far away from the Cultural Centre stands the family house of Makarios in which he was born and bred before leaving for Kykko monastery. It is a vey simple and poor traditional mountain house. The whole village of Panagia impresses with its traditional architecture, the climbing vines in front of the entrance doors, the large red wine jars currently decorating courtyards and the centuries-old oak-trees.

The busts of Mouskos and Sofocleous, at the entrance to the Gymnasium, point out the sacrifice of another two youths in the Cypriot struggle for Liberation. Close to the Gymnasium stands the large church of Agios Georgios, three-aisled, in which are preserved some very old portable icons. The restored church dates back to the 17th century. Worth visiting is the steep-pitched medieval chruch of B.V.M. Eleousa, at the periphery of the settlement, built with beams inside and flat tiles on the roof. The church is without mural paintings while the iconostasis is worn out. According to tradition, the original settlement of Panagia was close to Kremmos tou Koukou on the road between Panagia and Chrysorrogiatissa monastery.

Chrysorrogiatissa Monastery, is situated on a slope of mount Rogia, about 800 metres a.s.l., west of Pafos forest. In front of the main entrance to the monastery there is a café/restaurant from where the view is extensive and majestic. The monastery was founded in 1152 A.D. by monk Ignatios who found at Moulia

Cultural centre of Panagia village

Chrysorrogiatissa Monastery

(Pafos) the miraculous icon of Panagia, believed to have been painted by St Luke the Evangelist. Ignatios took the icon to the mountain where is now the monastery. Very little is known of Chrysorrogiatissa between the 12th century and the date Cyprus was conquered by the Turks (1571). At some time administratively it belonged to Kykko monastery. Barsky, the Russian monk, who visited the monastery in the 18th century, describes it as "poor, administered by Kykko, but located on a picturesque site, cool in summer with healthy water".

At the end of the 18th century the monastery was restored, with the single-aisled church being built on the foundations of the older one. A school, functioning for the children of the neighbouring villages since the middle of the 18th century, was dissolved at the end of the 19th century. The church in the middle of the monasterial complex, impressess with the frescoes above the three entrances. In the vaulted church there are no frescoes except one in the sanctum depicting the Sacrifice of Abraham. The icon of Panagia Chrysorrogiatissa, with the exception of the face of Virgin Mary, is silver-and gold-covered since the 18th century. Even the fire of 1967 did not destroy the gilted iconostasis nor some other valuable treasures of the monastery (holy Gospels, manuscripts, crosses, silver reliquaries etc) kept for centuries.

A Byzantine Hagiographic Centre has recently been set up for the protection of Byzantine and post-Byzantine icons as well as other treasures. A winery has also been established in the monastery in 1985 producing good quality wines from the vineyards of the monastery. The fermentation is done under natural conditions, without the intervention of modern technology. It is worth buying a bottle of wine from the Monastery.

Between Chrysorrogiatissa monastery and the new, planned settlement of Statos-Agios Fotios, stands the historic **Monastery of Agia Moni** or Monastery of Agios Nikolaos or the Monastery of Priests, because of the large number of priests/monks it hosted in the past.

According to tradition, the monastery was

153

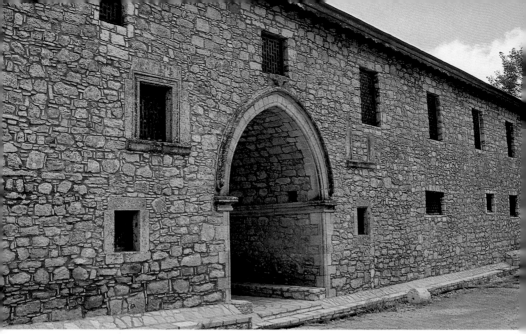

Monastery of Agia Moni

built by St Evtychios and St Nikolas, in the 4th century A.D., on the ruins of the temple of Hera.

In the 12th century the monastery possessed a workshop of manuscript-copying, while during the Frankish period it possessed three annexes. It was during the Turkish occupation of Cyprus that it declined and became an annex of Kykko monastery. In 1752, when Kykko monastery was destroyed by fire, the holy icon of the Madonna of Kykko was transferred, for safety purposes, here. In 1820, the monastery was, however, abandoned.

The entrance to the restored monastery is through an arched door with an inscription on the left side pointing out that the monastery was restored in 1696. The shape of the monastery is the normal four-sided structure with the church on the fourth side.

The present church is two-aisled with the northern aisle supported by arches. From the description of the Russian monk, Barsky, it might have been three-aisled,

domed, built on the ruins of an older Byzantine church. Even the Byzantine church was built on the ruins of a palaio-Byzantine church. Currently, it is built with hewn limestone blocks, while its icons are modern. A few metres north of the main church is a cruciform chapel, probably originally Latin, which is oriented north and south, not east and west. The monastery is situated in a unique position with extensive view. Currently, and particularly as from 1993, Agia Moni is a convent.

Statos-Agios Fotios, a planned settlement of 1974, is also known as *Ampelitis.* The earthquakes of 1953 and particularly the landslides of 1961, 1962, 1966, 1967, 1968 and 1969 were the main factors which compelled the Government to transfer the settlements of Statos and Agios Fotios to the new site which is caled Statos-Agios Fotios after the names of both villages.

However, the villagers continue to visit their scattered properties in the original villages. Trees, particularly walnut-trees have been planted along both sides of the new wide roads. The church of Our Saviour, in the middle of the settlement, dominates the landscape. Currently, a winery operates in the village. The private family house of Archbishop Chrysostomos lies on a conspicuous rise.

Statos is currently an abandoned settlement lying north-west of present-day Statos-Agios Fotios. A few years ago there were many stills in the village for the production of zivania. According to N. Klerides, in antiquity there was a military station at the village called Statos. Most probably this dates back to the Roman times.

Agios Fotios, lying south-west of present-day Statos-Agios Fotios, is currently abandoned. The traditional architecture of the deserted village is, however, still impressive. Hogarth mentions the pierced stones of Agios Fotios which are among the earliest discovered in Cyprus.

MANACHILAKA PICNIC SITE

It is situated 2 km from Panagia towards Kykkos. It has a capacity of 600 persons. It is equipped with car parking, toilets, piped drinking water, tables and benches, barbecue facilites and children's play areas.

---

b) The Mountainous villages

Destination: Stavros tis Psokas

The visitor can approach Stavros tis Psokas either through Lysos or through Agyia (Agyia picnic site has already been described see p.120). The route via Panagia is rather long to be recommended. Though the distances on the map appear to be short, nevertheless, the time required is rather long, since the traveller has to follow earthen, meandering, often narrow roads.

The roads are, however, hard and resistant, as they lie on igneous rocks.

Moufflon, living mainly in the forest of Pafos

The dominant forest tree throughout the route is the pine and the golden oak. Wild olive trees appear in some areas while the plane trees grow in deep valleys. On the way to Stavros tis Psokas the traveller might be lucky to meet groups of moufflon.

Stavros tis Psokas is a forest settlement, with tiled, steep pitched houses made of wood, including guest houses for those who would like to spend a few nights in the Station. In such case one should contact, by phone, the Divisional Forest Officer of Stavros beforehand (tel:26352324). At Stavros there are all facilities for a picnic including equipment for barbecue, while a restaurant caters for those who might like to stay overnight or those who have no time to enjoy the picnic site.

The environment at Stavros, amid the lush vegetation of pines, chestnut and cypress trees, next to cedar, golden oak and maple is very pleasant and cool, particularly in the warm summer days. Water from a natural spring is cold. At Stavros there is a nursery where seedlings of pine, cedar, fir etc, are produced for areas of Cyprus with the same relief and micro-climate. In an enclosure the visitor can see the moufflon, the national animal of Cyprus. A few deer, kept for acclimatization in enclosures at Stavros, can also be seen. They are beautiful, fast-running animals with the males having deciduous branching antlers. The deer, as historically known, used to live in Cyprus up to the Middle Ages. They were abundant in almost all the forests of Cyprus.

Stavros Nature Trails

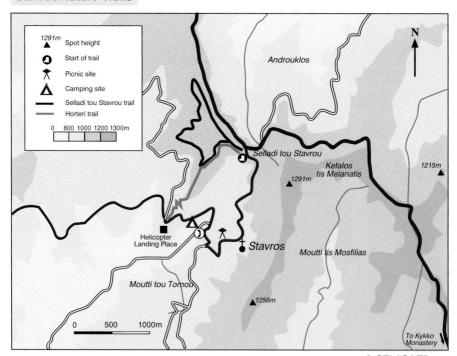

© SELAS LTD

Moufflon. Moufflon is as old as the first inhabitants of Cyprus or the first neolithic settlements of the island. In Neolithic times it was hunted and caught for its meat as well as for its bones. Later on, particularly in the Hellenistic-Roman times, its presence is testified to by the mosaics of Pafos. In the Middle Ages it was the game of the noble Frankish ruling class. In 1939, the forest of Pafos, where the animals live, was declared a game reserve area. The Turkish invasion of 1974 had restricted the animals to very low numbers, while currently it is believed that there are a few thousand. The emblem of the Cyprus Airways is the Cypriot moufflon, which is unique in the world. Though in the past moufflons could be encountered in the Troodos forest, currently they are confined mainly to the forest of Pafos. There is a seasonal movement to higher areas of the forest in summer and to lower in winter. Its pale brown hair protects it from enemies, as it resembles the colour of the natural vegetation. The moufflon belongs to the sheep family with the male having horns like those of a ram, and the female bearing no horns. The animals live from 15 to 20 years, are very elegant and powerful. As soon as they feel the presence of man they disappear. Normally they appear in groups of five or six.

STAVROS TIS PSOKAS PICNIC SITE

It is situated about 20 km from Lysos or Kannaviou village to Stavros valley, on the right hand side of the road, next to the forest station of Stavros tis Psokas. It has a capacity of about 600 persons. It is equipped with car parking, toilets, piped drinking water, tables and benches, barbecue facilities and children's play areas.

AVAILABLE IN STAVROS TIS PSOKAS

Cafeteria/Restaurant
Camping site
Hostel/Guest House
Moufflon enclosure
Natural trail
Picnic site

Stavros tis Psokas Nature Trails

There are two recommended nature trails in the area. *(See Map p.156)*

1. Selladi tou Stavrou. The trail starts from Selladi tou Stavrou and its length is 2,6 km. The walk time is approximately 1 hour. It is a circular trail which ends up at the starting point.

2. Horteri Trail. The trail starts from "Platanouthkia" site on the Stavros tis Psokas-Selladi tou Stavrou road. The length of the trail is 5 km and the walk time is approximately 2 hours.

Destination: Chapel of Agios Georgios Emnon

About 10 km north-west of Panagia stands the steep-pitched chapel of Agios Georgios Emnon, constructed in 1978 with local building meterial.

The chapel, built by the Presidential guard, in memory of the late president Makarios, is simple without mural paintings. It is built amid centuries-old pine-trees on the ruins of an original church dedicated to St George. The freshness of the forest, the murmuring of the pine-trees, the caress of the breeze and the singing of endemic and migratory birds constitute important components of the environment. Numerous aromatic plants grow around the church while in spring the area is flooded with colours and scents.

It is in this solitude that Makarios spent many days and probably nights in his youth, close to his father's sheepfold. He

Road between Panagia and Cedar valley

must have been affected by this lonely atmosphere. The chapel can be approached either by asphalted road from Panagia or through earthen road from Kykko.

Visits to the Kykko monastery through the Forest of Pafos

Very often local and foreign tourists wish to visit the historic Kykkos monastery (in Nicosia district). The forest of Pafos can be crossed by two routes:

(a) Through Stavros tis Psokas. This route follows Sellain tou Skotomenou (with cool water), Dodeka Anemoi with Tripylos 1362 m. a.s.l. on your right, and Matsimas (with piped cool water), before you reach Kykkos monastery.

The visitor who chooses this route will observe the efforts of the Department of Forest to reforest burnt areas on steep slopes and deep valleys and ravines. The flora is rich, while the pictures are abundant, rare and aesthetically attractive.

(b) Through Panagia. This route, among variations of green, passes by the chapel of Agios Georgios Emnon (it has already been described), built in memory of late Archbishop Makarios. This is a quiet nice spot with piped water to rest. Soon the traveller crosses the Valley of Cedars with the beautiful cedar trees occupying a vast area. The cedars appear as carpets, over-shadowing everything underneath. It is a superb spectacle worth enjoying before continuing the trip. The rest of the trip is among steep-sided valleys, ridges and tree-clad slopes, before the historic and most renowned monastery of Cyprus is encountered.

USEFUL INFORMATION

Cyprus is the largest island of the eastern Mediterranean. It is an independent Sovereign Republic with a presidential system of Government.

Area: 9.251 sq km
Latitude: 34° 33' - 35° 34' N
Longitude: 32° 16' - 34° 37' E

(Since 1974, 37,5% of Cyprus is occupied by the Turkish troops)

Population (de jure): 778.700 (2006 est.) of which:
76,1% Greek Cypriots
10,2% Turkish Cypriots
13,7% other minorities (Maronites, Armenians, Latins, etc.).

Population of main towns (2006):
Nicosia: 228.400
Limassol: 180.100
Larnaka: 80.400
Pafos: 54.000

Languages: Greek is the main language in the free part of Cyprus, with English spoken everywhere. French and German are also spoken.

Other Facts (2006)

Population in government controlled areas	601,7
Exports (€ million)	1.112
Imports (€ million)	5.514
Tourist arrivals	2.401
Hotel capacity-incl. apartments (beds)	93.957
Foreign exchange receipts from tourism (€ million)	1.755
Public roads (km)	11.976
Crude Birth rate (1000 pop)	11,3
Crude Death Rate (1000 pop)	6,7
G.N.P. per capita (CY £) (1996)	7.082
Density of population per km	81,2
Persons per doctor	384
Persons per dentist	1041
Persons per hospital bed	266
Telephones/100 population	49,5
Persons per private saloon car	2,1
Passenger cars/1000 population	430,3
Life expectancy at birth: females	79,8
males	75,0

☐ PUBLIC HOLIDAYS

1 January: New Year's Day. This is a very significant day for the Greek Cypriots who celebrate the New Year's Eve with drinking, singing, dancing, or playing cards. People in towns and especially in villages attend church in the morning of the New Year's Day.

6 January: Epiphany Day. In seaside towns and some big villages after the morning service, either the bishop or the priest heads a procession to the sea where the water is blessed. A cross is thrown into the sea where young divers swim to find it.

Green Monday or Clean Monday: This day is celebrated forty days before Easter Day. It is the beginning of Lent and almost everybody goes out to the countryside to picnic.

Carnival Day: It takes place some days before the beginning of the Lent. People in Limassol and to a lesser extent Pafos as well as in other towns and some big villages parade in the main streets disguised and dressed in fancy costumes.

25 March: It is a major Greek national day as well as an important religious holiday.

1 April: It is a Cypriot National Day with secondary school pupils as well as students of higher institutes attending church service.

Easter Day (March/April): It is the most important holiday for the Greek Cypriots with a solemn mass and chanting on Good Friday night, with a midnight service on Saturday accompanied by fireworks and with a church service on Sunday mid-day. During Sunday in towns and on Monday and Tuesday in most villages, apart from the cracking of the red eggs, traditional dancing and various local games are carried out. Good Friday, Good Saturday as well as Monday after Easter are public holidays.

1 May: The first day of May is not only celebrated by workers but by all Cypriots, being a public holiday.

15 August: It is a religious holiday for the Greek Cypriots.

1 October: It is the Day of Cypriot Independence, celebrated with military parade in the main towns of Cyprus, particularly in Nicosia, before the President of the Republic and other Officials.

28 October: It is an important Greek National Day, well-known as "Ochi" or "No" day, because on that day the Greeks refused Mussolini's demand in 1940 to enter Greek territory. Veterans as well as school pupils parade in the streets carrying Greek flags as well as their school banners.

25 December (Christmas Day): A religious holiday for the Greek Cypriots. The 26th of December is also a public holiday.

Note: *Most of the Greek orthodox religious days are also public holidays for the rest of the Christian minorities in Cyprus, like the Armenians, Catholics etc.*

All public services and most of the private enterprises and shops are closed on public holidays.

CHURCHES AND MONASTERIES

As the Byzantine churches have unique icons and frescoes they are locked. If you wish to visit any of these churches we recommend you to ask at the kafeneion (coffee shop) of the village for the priest or any other responsible person who could open the church for you. While visiting the churches and monasteries you should avoid to wear shorts or short dresses.

Most of the Monasteries have visiting hours usually from 09:30 or 10:00-16:00 hrs from Nov.-May and 10:00-18:00 from June-October.

PLACES OF WORSHIP IN PAFOS

Greek Orthodox Churches
Masses: Saturday: 18.30' - 19.15'
Sunday: 06.15' - 09.15'

Anglican Masses
Chrysopolitissa church/Agia Kyriaki, Kato Pafos.
Tel: c/o 26953044
Services: Sunday: 8:30 hrs &18.00 hrs
            Wed.: 9:00 hrs

Roman Catholic Masses
Chrysopolitissa Church/Agia Kyriaki, Kato Pafos.
Tel: 26931308
Masses: Sunday 10:00 hrs (Latin), 11:00 hrs (German, Polish), 12:00 hrs (English), Sat: 18:00 hrs.
At St. Nicholas Church, Polis. C/o tel: 26931308
Masses: Sunday 10:00 hrs

Carnival parade

The holy ceremony of the burial of Christ during Easter

German Evangelical Church
Agia Kyriaki/Chrysopolitissa Church, Kato Pafos.
Masses: Every second Saturday of the month at
16:00 hrs (Sep.-June)

⬜ ARCHAEOLOGICAL SITES & MUSEUMS

All museums and archaeological sites are closed
on the 25th of December (Christmas), New Year's
Day and Easter Sunday (Greek Orthodox).

Most of the archaeological sites are open from
09:00-17:00 hrs (09:00-19:30 hrs in Summer).
Opening hours are various (check on pages 54-
55 the opening hours for each museum
separately). During the Summer period the
archaeological sites stay open longer. Every
Sunday there is free admittance for all European
citizens to all State Museums and archaeological
sites.

The Pafos District Archaeological Museum
53, Georgiou Griva Digeni Str., 8100,
Tel: 26306215

Byzantine Museum
Joined to the Bishopric building (near Ag.
Theodoros church), 7, Andrea Ioannou Str.,
8047, Tel: 26931393

Ethnographical Museum
1, Exo Brysis Str., 8047,
Tel: 26932010

Pafos Mediaeval Fort
Kato Pafos-harbour area

Pafos Municipal Art Gallery
7, Gladstonos Str.,
Tel: 26930653

Tombs of the Kings
Kato Pafos
Tel: 26306295

Pafos Mosaics
Kato Pafos
Tel: 26306217

Geroskipou Folk Art Museum
3 km east of Pafos, Archbishop Makarios III Ave.,
& Leontiou Str., 8200,
Tel: 26306216

Sanctuary of Aphrodite-Palaipafos Museum
14 km east of Pafos, 8500, Kouklia Village
Tel: 26432180

*Museum of the Mycenaean Colonisation of
Cyprus*
Maa-Palaiokastro (Coral Bay area)

Archaeological site of Ag. Georgios Pegeia
Ag. Georgios, Pegeia Village area

Archaeological Museum of Marion-Arsinoe
26, Leoforos Makariou III, Polis
Tel: 26322955

Byzantine Museum of Arsinoe
c/o Bishopric of Arsioe, Peristerona Village,
9 km South of Polis
Tel: 26352515

Fyti-Weaving Museum
Fyti Village
C/o Tel: 26732126

Drouseia-Weaving Museum
Drouseia Village
Tel: 26332561

Kato Akourdaleia-Folk Art Museum
Kato Akourdaleia Village
Tel: 26306216

Basket Weaving Museum-Ineia Folk Art Museum
8704, Ineia Village
Tel: 26332562

◻ ACCOMMODATION

In Pafos the tourist can find a variety of accommodation from modern and luxurious hotels to small and cheap tourist apartments. Most Hotels and Hotel Apartments have swimming pools, sport facilities like tennis courts and other amenities.

All the accommodation establishments are listed in the "Guide to Hotels and other Tourist establishments" published by the Cyprus Tourism Organisation and are listed by type, category and class. The Cyprus Tourism Organisation (CTO) has offices in all towns and Larnaka International Airport, Pafos International Airport & Lemesos Harbour.

1. Hotels: Hotels are classified by the Cyprus Tourism Organisation in categories ranging between "five stars" ***** and "one star" *. You can find below some selected hotels all over Cyprus ranging in various price categories. The prices given below are listed in the "Guide to Hotels and other Tourist Establishments" published by the C.T.O. in 2007 and concern a double room including breakfast. However, there are off season discount rates which can reach 30% in some cases.

Pafos:

Annabelle ***** Poseidon Ave.,
Tel: 26938333, price: €132,00

Azia Beach ***** Akamas Rd, Chlorakas
Tel: 26845100, price: €246,00

Elysium Beach Resort ***** Queen Verenikis Str.,
Tel: 26844444, price: €246,00

Leptos Coral Beach ***** Coral Bay
Tel: 26881000, price: €325,00

Pafos Amathous Beach ***** Poseidon Ave.,

Tel: 26883300, price: €342,00

Venus Beach ***** Tombs of the Kings Rd.,
Tel: 26949200, price: €207,00

Alexander the Great **** Poseidon Ave.,
Tel: 26965000, price: €183,00

Almyra **** Poseidon Ave.,
Tel: 26933091, price: €208,00

Aloe **** Poseidon Ave.,
Tel: 26964000, price: €227,00

Aquamare Beach **** Poseidon Ave.,
Tel: 26966000, price: €167,00

Ascos Beach **** Pegeia,
Tel: 26621801, price: €170,00

Athena Beach **** Poseidon Ave.,
Tel: 26884600, price: €180,00

Athena Royal Beach **** Poseidon Ave.,
Tel: 26884600, price: €172,00

Ledra Beach **** Theas Aphrodites Ave.,
Geroskipou, Tel: 26964848, price: €188,00

Luca-Cypria Laura Beach **** Chlorakas,
Tel: 26944900, price: €168,00

St. George **** Chlorakas,
Tel: 26845000, price: €176,00

The Pioneer Beach **** Poseidon Ave.,
Geroskipou, Tel: 26964500, price: €171,00

Agapinor *** 24, Nikodimou Mylona Str.,
Tel: 26933926, price: €98,00

Cynthiana Beach *** Kisonerga,
Tel: 26933900, price: €113,00

Leptos Pafos Gardens *** Kleious Str.,
Tel: 26882000, price: €160,00

Paphian Bay *** Poseidon Ave., Geroskipou,
Tel: 26964333, price: €133,00

Queen's Bay *** Kisonerga,
Tel: 26946600, price: €120,00

Theofano *** Danais Str.,
Tel: 26965700, price: €163,00

Polis:

Anassa ***** Neo Chorio,
Tel: 26888000, price: €307,00

Natura Beach *** Polis,
Tel: 26323111, price: €104,00

Marion ** Marion Str.,
Tel: 26321216, price: €116,00

Drouseia

Cyprotel Droushia Heights *** Drouseia,
Tel: 26332351, price: €82,00

Kouklia

Intercontinental Aphrodite Hills Resort,
Aphrodite Ave., Kouklia
Tel: 26829000, price: €243,00

2. Hotel Apartments : Hotel Apartments are also classified by the Cyprus Tourism Organisation in categories ranging between "A" to "C"

Pafos:

Anemi CLASS "A", Kikeronos Str.,
Tel: 26945666, price: €106,00

Corallia Beach CLASS "A", Coral Bay,
Tel: 26622121, price: €102,00

Demetra CLASS "A", 4, Artemis Str.,
Tel: 26934444, price: €77,00

Helios Bay CLASS "A", Chlorakas,
Tel: 26935656, price: €85,00

Mayfair CLASS "A", Pari Str.,
Tel: 26948000, price: €85,00

Hilltop Gardens CLASS "B", Off Tombs of the Kings Rd., Tel: 26943111, price: €65,00

Pafos Gardens Narkissus CLASS "C",
Kleious Str., Tel: 26882000, price: €154,00

Polis:

Andreas Tavros CLASS "A", Neo Chorio,
Tel: 26322421, price: €68,00

Bougenvilea CLASS "B", 13, Verginas Str.,
Tel: 26812250, price: €62,00

Stefanos CLASS "B", 8, Arsinois Str.,
Tel: 26322411, price: €77,00

3. Tourist Apartments

4. Tourist villas (luxury, A,B,C class)

5. Tourist villages (A&B class)

Pafos:

Aliathon CLASS "A", Poseidonos Ave., Geroskipou
Tel: 26964400, price: €99,00

Aqua Sol CLASS "A", Pegeia,
Tel: 26622200, price: €108,00

Polis:

Elia Latchi Holiday Village CLASS "A", Polis,
Tel: 26321011, price: €126,00

6. Traditional Holiday Homes: In some villages traditional houses have been restored in order to accommodate tourists and offer a new experience of holidaying. They are all fully equipped with all modern comforts. You can find traditional holiday homes in many villages such as in Kritou Tera (Pafos), Kato Akourdaleia (Pafos), Kathikas (Pafos), P. Arodes (Pafos), Tochni (Larnaka), Kalavasos (Larnaka), Arsos (Limassol), Lofou (Limassol) etc.

ELIA LATCHI HOLIDAY VILLAGE

Holidays just for you!

For those who like rest, tranquility and relaxation.
For those who like to enjoy both the sea and the greenery of the Countryside.
For those who wish to offer their children and friends the best.
Latchi has much to commend. For culinay delights Latchi offers fresh fish
and in the beautiful atmosphere of our Holiday Village we offer:

- *3 Swimming pools (2 outdoors and 1 indoor)*
- *Bars*
- *Taverna with special nights reflecting different culture and cuisine*
- *3 Tennis courts*
- *Squash*
- *Minigolf*

- *Football pitch with grass*
- *Basket-ball court*
- *Volley-ball court*
- *Archery*
- *Children club with animation programme*
- *Music every night with a variety of animation programme*

or information and reservation please call: Tel. 26322021, Fax 26322024

Huge signposts with place-names indicated in Greek and Roman script.

Properties in Pafos:

Pafos is an ideal place for holiday makers and many visitors wish to get a property here.

There are many cypriot property companies who sell quality properties in Pafos District at competitive prices.

You can find in Pafos a variety of houses and apartments, luxury villas and bungalows. They are suitable for holiday homes, permanent living and investment. All property companies can advise you on the best options to choose.

7. Rest Houses:

-There is a Rest House at Stavros tis Psokas Forest station in the Pafos Pine forest.
Tel: 26999144/26352324

8. Camping

- *Geroskipou Zenon Gardens Camping*

	Nicosia	Larnaka	Larnaka Airport	Limassol	Pafos	Pafos Airport	Agia Napa	Parali-mni	Troodos	Pano Platres	Agros	Polis
Nicosia		44	48	81	147	137	75	75	69	74	53	179
Larnaka	44		4	66	132	122	40	40	112	101	99	164
Larnaka Airport	48	4		70	136	126	44	44	116	105	103	168
Limassol	81	66	70		66	56	103	103	42	35	33	98
Pafos	147	132	136	66		13	172	172	56	54	99	32
Pafos Airport	137	122	136	56	13		162	162	46	44	89	45
Agia Napa	75	40	44	103	172	162		6	152	141	138	204
Paralimni	75	43	47	106	172	162	6		152	141	139	204
Troodos	69	112	116	42	56	46	152	152		5	18	87
Pano Platres	74	101	105	35	54	44	141	141	5		24	82
Agros	53	99	103	33	99	89	139	139	18	24		131
Polis	179	164	168	98	32	45	204	204	87	82	131	

Distance chart (in km)   © SELAS

Situated at about 3 km from Pafos harbour.
Tel: 99632229
Open from April to October.

- Feggari Camping
Situated 16 km from Pafos town near the Coral
Bay beach. Tel: 26621534
Open all the year round.

- Polis Camping site
Situated on the beach at 500 metres from Polis
and 37 km from Pafos town.
Tel: 26815080. Open from March to October.

- Stavros tis Psokas Camping
Situated 20 km from Lysos or Kannaviou villages
near Stavros Forest Station.

9. Picnic sites

There are quite a few picnic sites in Pafos district.

- Agios Merkourios, is situated 7 km from Lysos
to Stavros tis Psokas, 4 km on the forest road
which leads to Agios Merkourios.

- Agyia, is situated 11 km north of Kannaviou on
the right hand site of the road.

- Gefyri tou Livadiou, is situated 13 km south of
Pomos towards Stavros tis Psokas Forest
Station.

- Manachilaka, is situated 2 km from Panagia
towards Kykkos.

- Mavralis, is situated 4 km from Polis towards
Agia Marina.

- Pera Vasa, is situated 9 km north of Agios
Nikolaos village after Kelefos Bridge.

- Pykni, is situated in Pegeia Forest, 3 km from
Pegeia on the road leading to Kathikas village.

- Smigies, is situated 2 km west of Neo Chorio
village in the Akamas Forest.

- Stavros tis Psokas, is situated about 20 km from
Lysos or Kannaviou in Stavros tis Psokas forest
station.

- Timi, is situated 1 km on the right hand site of
the road leading from Pafos International Airport
to Timi village.

☐ TRANSPORTATION

Visitors may enter the Republic of Cyprus
through the International airports of Larnaka and
Pafos and the ports of Larnaka and Limassol.

1. Airports
The International Airport of Larnaka is 48 km from
Nicosia town, 4 km from Larnaka town, 70 km
from Limassol, 44 km from Agia Napa and 136
km from Pafos. The International Airport of Pafos
is 137 km from Nicosia, 13 km from Pafos town,
56 from Limassol town, 122 km from Larnaka
and 45km from Polis.

Airlines
More than 30 airlines operate scheduled flights
to and from Larnaka International Airport and
Pafos International Airport.

Passengers are kindly requested to make their
reconfirmation of flights at least three days before
their departure.

Besides the airlines, travel agencies in Cyprus
provide booking services and assist visitors in
all matters concerning air travel.

2. Bus Service

Various Bus Companies operate between the
main towns and various holiday resorts.

Urban and suburban buses operate frequently
only during the day between 05.30 and 19.00 hrs.

Sightseeing Tours:

Guided excursions are organised by sightseeing
tour operators and include transportation in
airconditioned coaches, services of guides and
visits to a great variety of interesting places of
the island. Reservations for excursions can be
made through the hotel receptions. Tourists are
normally picked up from their hotels.

Normally village medieval churches and other
village monuments are closed.

The community priest or some other person can
provide the visitor with the key or can open the
door for him free of charge. If you conduct a visit

Picnic sites, Camping, Fishing

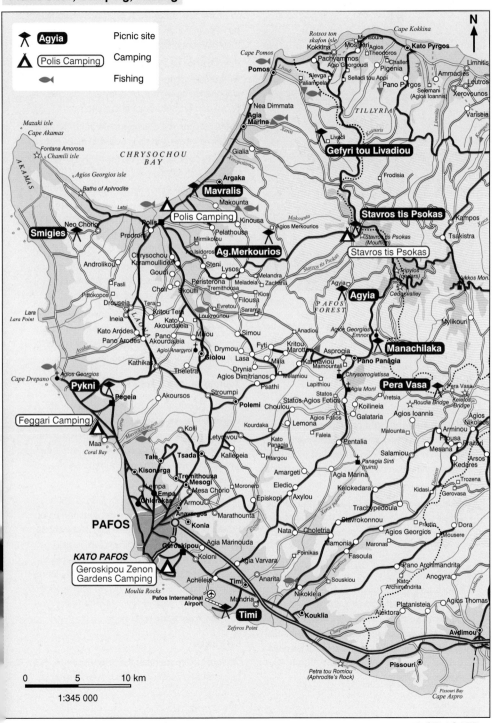

Legend:
- ⚘ **Agyia** — Picnic site
- ⛺ **Polis Camping** — Camping
- 🐟 — Fishing

N

Cape Kokkina
Rotsos ton skafon isle
Kokkina
Mosfileri
Agios Theodoros
Kato Pyrgos
Cape Pomos
Pachyammos
Limnitis
Pomos
Agio Giorgoudi
Challeri
Ammadies
Livadi
Pigenia
Loutros
Alevga
Selladi tou Appi
Xerovounos
Paliampela
Pano Pyrgos
Selemani
(Agios Ioannis)
Nea Dimmata
TILLYRIA
Variseia
Agia Marina
Xeros
Gialia
Livadi
Gefyri tou Livadiou
Makounta
Frodisia
CHRYSOCHOU BAY
Xeropotamos
Argaka
Makounta
Kampos
Mavralis
Makounta
Xeros
Mazaki isle
Cape Akamas
Fontana Amorosa
Chamili isle
Baths of Aphrodite
Agios Georgios isle
Kinousa
Stavros tis Psokas
Tsakistra
Polis Camping
Agios Merkourios
Stavros tis Psokas
(Moufflon)
Stavros tis Psokas
Latsi
Pelathousa
Neo Chorio
Polis
Mirmikofou
Prodromi
Agios Merkourios
Smigies
Stavros tis Psokas
Chrysochou
St. Isidoros
Tripylos
Karamoullides
Steni
(cedars)
Androlikou
Ag.Merkourios
Melandra
Kykkos Mon.
Goudi
Lysos
Meladeia
Zacharia
Cedar Valley
Periastona
Tremithousa
Choli
Skoulli
Kios
Agyia
Myllkouri
Pittokopos
Filousa
Agyia
Drouseia
Tera
Evretou
Saramã
Fasli
Kritou Tera
Loukrounou
PAFOS FOREST
Lara
Kato
Ineia
Akourdaleia
Simou
Agios Georgios Emnon
Lara Point
Pano
Kato Arodes
Akourdaleia
Miliou
Anadiou
Pano Arodes
Agioi Anargyroi
Kritou
Manachilaka
Marottou
Drymou
Fyti
Asprogia
Kathikas
Siolou
Lasa
Milia
Pano Panagia
Avakas
Theletra
Drynia
Karmiaviou
Mamountali
Cape Drepano
Agios Georgios
Melanaiou
Agios Dimitrianos
Chrysorrogiatissa
Pera Vasa
Pykni
Akoursos
Stroumpi
Psathi
Lapithiou
Agia Moni
Pera Vasa
Pegeia
Statos
Kelefos
Statos-Agios Fotios
Koilineia
Roudia Bridge
Bridge
Feggari Camping
Choulou
Vretsia
Agios
Koili
Agios Fotios
Galataria
Nikolaos
Maa
Kourdaka
Lemona
Malounta
Arminou
Coral Bay
Letymvou
Kato
Faleia
Pentalia
Frousa
Praitori
Tala
Tsada
Panagia
Salamiou
Mesana
Kallepeia
Pitargou
Arsos
Kisonerga
Tremithousa
Moronero
Amargeti
Panagia Sinti
Kidasi
Kedares
Mesogi
Mesa Chorio
(ruins)
Trozena
Lempa
Empa
Armou
Eledio
Agia Marina
Gerovasa
Ohlorakas
Axylou
Kelokedara
Anavargos
Marathounta
Episkopi
Trachypedoula
PAFOS
Konia
Prastio
Nata
Choletria
Stavrokonnou
Dora
Geroskipou
Agia Marinouda
Mamonia
Agios Georgios
Mousere
KATO PAFOS
Koloni
Maronas
Pano Archimandrita
Anogyra
Geroskipou Zenon Gardens Camping
Agia Varvara
Foinikas
Fasoula
Kato
Archimandrita
Acheleia
Timi
Anarita
Souskiou
Agios Thomas
Moulia Rocks
Mandria
Nikoklea
Platanisteia
Pafos International Airport
Alektora
Avdimou
Timi
Kouklia
Chapotami
Zefyros Point
Petra tou Romiou
(Aphrodite's Rock)
Pissouri
Pissouri Bay
Cape Aspro

0   5   10 km

1:345 000

Sea sports

Visitors can drive in Cyprus provided they possess either an international driving licence or their national driving licence.

Petrol can be bought at numerous petrol stations within the towns or in many villages. Petrol stations are open from Monday to Friday (6a.m-6p.m) and on Saturdays (6a.m - 4p.m).

Petrol stations are equipped with petrol vending machines where service is available for 24 hours.

Traffic in Cyprus moves on the left hand-side of the road and NOT on the right.International road traffic signs are in use and are placed along the roads and highways, on the left hand-side. The road speed, unless otherwise indicated, is 100 km on the motorways and 80 km on all other roads unless a different one is indicated.

In the urban areas the road speed is 50 km, unless otherwise indicated. Seat belts for front and back seat passengers is compulsory.

Car Rentals - Hire Cars: Self drive cars known as "Z cars", because their number plates are marked by a "Z", can be hired by many car rental firms all over Cyprus at reasonable prices.

Touring Guides & Tourist Maps

Selas (Center of Studies, Research & Publications) has already published high quality touring guides of Cyprus, Agia Napa-Protaras-Paralimni, Larnaka (town and countryside), Limassol, Pafos (town and countryside) Nicosia (Greater Urban area) etc.

The Road & Tourist map of Cyprus (1:250000), pubished by SELAS, is very detailed and of top quality with over 8.000 entries and explanations. SELAS has the largest collection of maps of all towns & districts in Cyprus (Nicosia, Limassol, Pafos, Larnaka, Agia Napa-Protaras-Paralimni) which are detailed up-to-date and very accurate road & tourist maps. For more information you can visit www.selas.com.cy

5. Cruises

Visitors to Cyprus have the opportunity to visit neighbouring countries in luxurious cruise ships.

on your own, without the services of a guide, be sure you ask for the key at the village central square or the kafeneion (café).

3. Taxi Service
Service taxis are available in the main towns. Transurban taxis operate from 06.00 - 18.30 (19.30 in summer) and provide connections between Nicosia and all towns. Seats are shared with other people and can be booked by phone. The passenger can be picked up from his home or hotel.

Urban taxis are available in Nicosia and can be booked by phone or be hired from their base station. Passengers are dropped at any place they wish.

4. Car Driving
Cyprus has fairly good asphalted roads complying with international traffic requirements, which link the main towns with villages. Four-lane motorways connect Nicosia with Limassol and Larnaka as well as Limassol with Larnaka, Larnaka with Agia Napa and Paralimni and Limassol with Pafos.

Welcome to www.selas.com.cy

COMPANY PROFILE

ROAD & TOURIST MAPS

POCKET MAPS

A-Z STREET ATLASES

SCHOOL ATLASES

WALL MAPS

TOURING GUIDES

TRAVEL BOOKS

GEOGRAPHY OF CYPRUS

CUSTOM MAPPING

ORDER FORM

CONTACT US

Road & Tourist Map of Cyprus

12th Revised Edition
Scale 1:250 000
Size 90x60 cm, folded.
Includes maps of Nicosia, Limassol, Larnaka, Pafos, Agia Napa-Protaras-Paralimni, Hill Resorts and Nature Trails and index to places of interest and hotels.

sample   Order

Road & Tourist Map of Pafos

7th Revised Edition
Size 92x67 cm, folded.
Includes street map of Pafos town (1:9 500), physical map of Pafos district (1:100 000), street map of Polis, map of Akamas & Stavros, Nature Trails, index to villages and hotels.

sample   Order

Road & Tourist Map of Pafos (Pocket)

Scale 1:8 000
Size 69x47 cm
Includes street map of Pafos town, index to all places of interest and hotels and street index.

sample   Order

Touring Guide of Cyprus

7th Revised Edition
Fully coloured
Size 21x15 cm
304 pages
256 colour photos
18 original maps

sample   Order

Cyprus

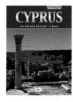

Size 26x19,5 cm
128 pages,
6 original maps,
176 colour photos.

sample   Order

Center of Studies, Research & Publications SELAS Ltd. Tel: 22336633, Fax: 22337033, P.O.Box: 28619, 2081, Nicosia, Cyprus. www.selas.com.cy, e-mail: selas@spidernet.com.cy

Travel agencies offer mini-cruises from Limassol port which include accommodation on board, meals and excursions to the main places of interest of each country.

There is a two-day cruise to the Holy Land, two-day cruise to Egypt, a three-day cruise to both Holy Land and Egypt and a seven-day cruise to Greece, Greek Islands and the Holy Land.

Prices vary according to the cabin category. The ships offer a great variety of facilities and entertainment including shows, casinos, swimming pools, duty free shops etc. Bookings can be made through travel agencies in all towns.

6. Boat Trips in Cyprus

From May to October, one-day cruises are organised with itineraries from Pafos Harbour to Coral Bay and from Polis (Latsi) along the Akamas coast.

The trips usually include drinks and snacks on board, with lunch served either on board or at sea-side restaurants.

7. Marinas

There are two Marinas in Cyprus, one in Limassol and one in Larnaka. For further information apply to St. Raphael Marina, tel:25636100 and Larnaka Marina, tel:24653110.

☐ SPORTS

Cyprus Car Rally attracts entries from many countries and includes champion drivers from all over the world.

Football is very popular with many stadia suitable for football playing.

Tennis courts exist in nearly all hotels while special tennis centres function in the town. There is a tennis court at Geroskipou Tourist Beach, 3 km east of Pafos Harbour, tel: 99620913.

Horse-riding is confined at the moment in Nicosia at Lapatsa Sporting Centre and in Limassol at Elias Country Club. Horses and ponies can be

Traditional folk dancing

hired in Troodos as well.

Cycling is encouraged by the excellent conditions prevailing in Cyprus as well as by the bicycle rental facilities available in the main towns and sea-side resorts.

Fishing is an exciting sport with fishing shelters all over Cyprus. Angling can also be enjoyed in dams provided a special license is obtained from the Fisheries Dept. of the Ministry of Agriculture and Natural Resources. For information contact tel: 22807830 (Nicosia), 25305543 (Limassol), 24304294 (Larnaka), 26306268 (Pafos).

Boating can be enjoyed by hiring a speed boat at many beaches.

Hiking is recommended for those who would like to explore the island's natural and cultural treasures. Natural trails can be found at Troodos, Akamas, Cape Gkreko, Stavros tis Psokas, Madari (near Agros village) and other places.

Bowling is available at Kykko Bowling Centre (Nicosia) , at Limassol Bowling Centre (Limassol) and at Aliathon Bowling Club (Pafos).

Golf is available at Tsada village (Pafos), at

Secret Valley, near Petra tou Romiou, 18 km east of Pafos and 49 km from Limassol and at Aphrodite Hills. For more information contact: Tsada Golf Club, tel: 26642774 and Aphrodite Hills, tel: 26828200.

Horse-racing is confined to Nicosia with race meetings taking place at weekends and Wednesdays.

Shooting in Cyprus is an exciting and popular sport with clubs in every town. The Nicosia Shooting Club is at Latsia, 8 km south-west of the town centre, tel: 22482660. The Limassol Shooting Club is near Pareklisia village near Elias Hotel Country Club, tel: 99495130. For the Larnaka Shooting Club please contact tel: 24530309. The Famagusta District Shooting Club is at Paralimni (off Paralimni - Sotira road), tel: 23827000. The Pafos Shooting Club is at Anatoliko, 12 km east of Pafos town, tel: 99632347.

Diving can be very fascinating as Cyprus is surrounded by crystal clear and unpolluted seas with water temperatures varying from 16-27 degrees centigrade. It is, however, forbidden to remove antiquities from the bottom of the sea.

Swimming is practised by nearly all tourists, since the sea around Cyprus with its extensive beaches offers excellent opportunities for swimming and sunbathing. On every beach red buoys indicate the swimmer's areas, where speed boats are not allowed to enter.

In Cyprus there are 52 beaches awarded the **Blue Flag.** The Blue Flag is annually awarded to Beaches that comply with a list of criteria ranging from water quality to environmental education and information to beach area management and safety. *(See Beaches with Blue Flag on the maps).*

Other sea sports. A full range of water sports like water-skiing, wind-surfing, sailing, canoing, pedalling, parascending, yachting etc. is offered by sea-sport centres in coastal town and resorts as well as by the major hotels.

Ski can be enjoyed only on the Troodos mountains in the period between January and March.

Aviation Sports. The Cyprus Aero Club offers opportunities with the necessary aircraft and ground facilities for such air sports as power flying, gliding, parachute jumping, hand-gliding and aeromodelling.

Folk dancing and music performances take place during local festivals and Cyprus evenings in restaurants and hotels. Special folk dancing schools can be found all over Cyprus.

❑ FOOD AND DRINK

There are numerous individual restaurants to satisfy all demands and peculiar tastes. Some provide meals for those who prefer their food as close to home as possible, while others provide excellent local dishes.

Food

Some favourite Greek dishes are enumerated below all of which are presented on the menus with an English, French or German translation.

Cyprus mezedes is a collection of hot and cold appetisers which is served in small dishes and can be a meal on its own. Normally one starts with taramosalata (fish roe paste),talatouri (yoghurt and cucumber), tachinosalata (sesame seed paste), hummous (chick-peas-olive oil and hot spices), halloumi (local cheese), normally fried smoked sausages, skewered lamb, sheftalia (barbecued mince-meats), dishes including sometimes snails, octopus in red wine and other fish specialities. Foreigners are fascinated by this collection of appetisers since they always find something new,tasty,exciting and definitely Cypriot.

However, for those who would not like to taste mezedes, though at least for once they are recommended, there are numerous other dishes which they can try.

Moussaka. Made of eggplants (aubergines), sliced potatoes, finely minced beef or pork and cream sauce is a favourite cypriot dish.

ZORBAS
SINCE 1975

Pastitso which is macaroni baked in the oven with bechamel sauce is a speciality of many Cypriot women, particularly in the countryside.

Koupepia made of stuffed vine leaves is quite often served in restaurants.

Afelia (fried pork pieces with coriander), stifado (braised beef and onions), Yiouvarlakia and avgolemono (meat ball soup), Ravioles (boiled cheese-filled pasta), Kanellonia (meat filled pancakes), Kolokythakia yemista (stuffed zucchini), Yemista (stuffed vegetables), are special Cypriot dishes in both restaurants as well at home.

Keftedes (meat balls) is a very popular Cypriot dish made of eggs, bread, grated and strained potatoes, parsley, finely minced beef or pork and other spices.

Kebab is also very popular served by all restaurants, made either by pork or lamb. The small pieces of meat are skewered and roasted over a charcoal fire and usually eaten in a pitta bread.

Kleftiko is very popular particularly in countryside restaurants and is made of lamb, cooked very slowly in sealed earthenware pots in the village ovens, which are beehive constructions, made with baked mud.

Choirino me kolokassi (Pork with taro), a speciality of certain seasons, is prepared by boneless stewing pork, thickly sliced celery, freshly ground black pepper, lemon and of course kolokassi (taro).

Soupa avgolemono. It is worthwhile trying this Cypriot soup, known as soupa avgolemono (egg and lemon soup) prepared with rice, chicken stock, eggs and lemon which by continuous stirring helps to heat up the egg mixture gradually and avoid curdling.

Special Cypriot desserts are recommended particularly for those with a sweet tooth. *Baklava* is a pastry made of cinamon and nuts, *kateifi* is a shredded nut pastry, *galatoboureko* is a custard pie, *dactyla* are ladies fingers, a pastry with nut filling and syrup, *Bourekia* me anari is a fried cheese pastry, while *soutzoukos* is a local speciality made of strings of almonds dipped into grape juice and allowed to dry.

Pork dishes & mezes

Since ancient times pork meat constituted a vital item in the Cypriot's diet. Up to the first decades of the century pigs were reared in nearly every rural household, to be slaughtered at Christmas time. Present-day pork is still highly regarded, cooked and processed in different forms:

(a) *Souvlakia,* small pieces of pork grilled on skewers over charcoal. It is regarded as the "national dish" of Cyprus.

(b) *Sheftalia,* a mixture of fresh minced pork, finely-chopped onion and parsley, grilled on the charcoal.

(c) *Afelia,* small pieces of pork, dipped in red wine with coriander.

(d) *Roast pork*

(e) *Pork chops*

(f) *Choiromeri,* a leg of pork, dipped in red wine for at least five weeks, pressed and smoked. It is usually served as mezze.

(g) *Lounza,* pork fillet, dipped in red wine, with coriander seed on top, pressed and smoked. It is fried or grilled in tiny slices.

(h) *Loukanika.* This is the Cypriot sausage, made of good quality meat often flavoured with the fruit of the lentisk bush. It is smoked or dried in the sun. This is the traditional rural sausage, not the factory sausage.

(i) *Salami,* is factory-made and is served as a mezze.

(j) *Zalatina,* recommended as a winter mezze, is a kind of jellied brawn, made from parts of the pig.

Cypriot Cheeses

Cheeses in Cyprus are made from sheeps', goats'

Cyprus "mezedes" (hot and cold appetisers with special dishes) ▶

or cows' milk, or from a mixture. Their history is lost in time with some villages and monasteries noted for cheeses of exceptional quality. Herebelow are enumerated some well-known Cypriot cheeses: (a) *Halloumi*. It is more or less the national cheese of Cyprus, the village-made dry and flaky, from either goats' or sheeps' milk or even from a mixture. The factory-made halloumi can be of cows' milk. It can be eaten freshly-made, it can be preserved in special pots for later use and it can be fried with eggs or it can be grilled. (b) *Anari*. It is soft, creamless cheese, available salted or unsalted, served either on its own or used in the making or pastries. It is also used as dried and grated for macaroni dishes. In some villages it is offered extremely fresh together with honey or sugar. (c) *Fetta*. It has a salty taste and crumbly texture and is normally served in salads. (d) *Kefalotyri*. It is a rather hard cheese, of excellent flavour with some holes. It is a rather expensive cheese. (e) *Village Easter Cheese*. This is a local cheese, moulded in small baskets, yellowish in colour, prepared in Easter time for use in flaounes, a special Easter cake.

Drinks

There is a great variety of wines, old and new, sweet and dry, white or red, locally produced as well as factory-made. Wine making in Cyprus is one of the oldest industries. Cyprus wines rank among the best in the world, often being awarded with gold and silver medals. *"Commandaria"*, a dessert type of wine, is unique in the world, bearing this name since the Middle Ages. There are four big wineries in Cyprus: ETKO, KEO, LOEL, SODAP as well as many small wineries recently established at Chrysorrogiatissa Monastery, Arsos, Agios Amvrosios, Anogyra, Pelendri, Koilani, Kathikas, Pafos etc.

Brandy is locally produced and is either served on its own or as brandy sour when it is mixed with lemon juice, bitters and soda water.

Ouzo is an aniseed-flavoured drink produced locally.

Cypriot handicraft

There are two excellent types of beer locally produced and very refreshing on hot days, *Carlsberg* and *KEO*.

In addition you can find in Cyprus all types of refreshments ranging from colas to lemonades and fresh fruit juices produced in Cyprus and recommended for the foreign tourists.

Restaurants and their price-lists are controlled by the Cyprus Tourism Organisation.

Lunch is normally served in restaurants between 12.00 and 14.30 o'clock and dinner from 19.00 o'clock till late in the evening.

Nightlife in Cyprus

There are many places where a visitor can enjoy his evening. Apart from the numerous restaurants, tavernas, fish taverns and pizzarias, there is a number of pubs for a drink or a snack with European atmosphere. Besides, cabarets, discos and several places with Greek and pop music can be found all over Cyprus.

□ SHOPPING

There is a great variety of shops to satisfy every taste. Shopping hours for the Winter period (Nov.

Cyprus Handicrafts

Lefkara handmade lace, embroideries, crochet and needlework. Woven cotton cloth in traditional Lefkoniko, Karpass and Phiti styles. Handwoven, traditional costumes, leather goods, silverware, copperware, pottery, mosaic, wood-carved items, baskets and other rush-made articles.

CYPRUS HANDICRAFT SERVICE
MINISTRY OF COMMERCE, INDUSTRY AND TOURISM

Lefkosia: 186, Athalassa Avenue, Tel:22305024
Lemesos: 25, Themidos Street, Tel: 25305118
Larnaka: 6, Cosma Lysioti Street, Tel: 24304327
Pafos: 64, Apostolou Pavlou Avenue, Tel: 26306243

1-March 31): Monday, Tuesday, Thursday, up to 19:00 hrs, Wednesday, up to 14:00 hrs, Friday up to 20:00 hrs, Sat. up to 15:00 hrs. Shopping hours for the Summer period (April 1-October 31): Monday, Tuesday, Thursday, up to 20:30 hrs, Wednesday, up to 14:00 hrs, Sat. up to 17:00 hrs. Summer afternoon recess (June 15-August 31) from 14:00-17:00 hrs.

Hints for Cyprus Souvenirs

Quite a lot of Cypriot products can be bought in Cyprus, either at large hotels or in shops, even at kiosks set up along the roadside. Many Cypriot artisans are renowned for their handicrafts - ceramics, basketry, weaving, wood carving, silver and copper products. Paying a visit to the *Cyprus Handicraft Service,* a non-profit organization which runs shops in Nicosia, Limassol, Larnaka and Pafos, the tourist will find a wide selection of products. One finds a great variety of basketry, particularly small portable baskets in decorative shapes, objects of brass, like candlesticks, ashtrays, trays etc, carpets and curtains of different patterns, a great variety of ceramics, often inspired by ancient Greek mythology, or functional wares from Kornos and Foini, or even glazed ceramics with pretty geometric patterns. The copperware is rich and varied with hand-crafted ware, including copper bowls, pots etc. Cyprus, particularly Lefkara and a few other villages produce a large variety of hand-made embroidery. As far as food is concerned the turkish-delights of Geroskipos and Lefkara are well-known. Olives and the special variety of cypriot cheese, halloumi, can be carried home, while there is a large variety of wines and liquers to choose.

From some jewellers the visitor can buy silver and gold pieces, while shoes, sandals, handbags, belts, wallets as well as other leather goods can be found in many shops. The foreign visitor can also buy Cypriot stamps and coins, wooden articles, woollen goods, like sweaters, shawls as well as woven goods. Some visitors prefer pyrographed or painted gourds, known in Cyprus as *"Kolokia"*. It is a vegetable of the marrow family hanging from plants often adorning verandahs and taverns. The gourds are decorated and sold as souvenirs. Not very many tourists buy stools made from anathrika, the fennel plant. An icon, often a copy of an original coloured icon, is another souvenir item worth considering. Besides, one can find cheap paintings and sculptures of Cypriot artists.

In Cyprus the tourist can purchase contact lenses, spectacle frames, sunglasses and other optical objects at relatively low prices.

The visitor might even consider a map of Cyprus (SELAS produces high quality maps), books on Cyprus, calendars of the island and so on.

Tax Free Shopping

As a foreign visitor you are entitled to claim back the tax you pay on your purchases when you take them home. The easy and safe way to reclaim your tax is with Global Refund, the world's leading tax refund company. This service is offered by major retailers world-wide. Note: All non EU citizens are entitled for VAT refund.

Your total purchases (VAT included) must exceed 50 Euro in a store from where you ask for a refund Cheque.

When leaving Cyprus (from either Larnaka or Pafos International Airports) you show your purchases and receipts to Customs officials. Your Global Refund Cheque must be stamped by Customs within 3 months plus a month of purchase.

☐ HEALTH MATTERS

Cyprus has a very healthy climate and water is safe to drink. Nevertheless you can find various types of cheap mineral water, particularly from the mountains of Cyprus, which you can drink either in glass or plastic bottles.

If mosquitoes are a problem, the tourist can use a mosquito coil or other devices especially if the window is open during night time.

It feels even better
when you shop Tax Free

As a non-European Union resident you are entitled to a tax refund when you shop for more than €50 in one store in one day. Global Refund, the world's leader in Tax Free Shopping services, allows you to receive a fast, simple and safe refund. Ask for Tax Free Shoping in the store. The more you spend, the greater the rewards.

Medical care is offered either by the Government hospitals or the private clinics. Government hospitals as well as some private clinics have casualty departments for emergency cases. Since medical facilities must be paid, tourists are advised to take out their private medical insurance. Almost all brands of medicines are available in Cyprus.

Private doctor's visiting hours on weekdays are 09.00-13.00 and 16.00-19.00.

Pharmacies

There is a significant number of pharmacies which are open during normal shopping hours. However, the daily press gives the names, addresses and telephone numbers of the pharmacies that stay open at night, on Sundays and public holidays.

In case of urgent problems by calling 11892 on the telephone you can get the information you want. Nearly all medicines sold in Europe are available but some of them require a prescription. Pharmacists can generally advise on minor problems such as sunburn, blisters, gastric disorters, throat infections, cuts etc.

☐ SUGGESTED CLOTHING

Some information concerning clothing during the whole year is afforded herebelow.

- *December - January:* It is the winter time for Cypriots, though sunshine is not absent, sometimes for protracted periods. Winter clothing, but definetely not heavy coats.

- *February - March:* Occasional rain with, sometimes, chilly evenings. Warm days are, however, a common phenomenon. March is a spring period. Winter clothing with medium-weight wear.

- *April - May:* Pleasantly warm days, though temperatures may fall a bit at night. Medium-weight and summer apparel, with woollies for the evenings.

- *June - July - August:* Summer time with warm temperatures. Very light-weight summer clothing.

- *September - October:* Warm days with cool October evenings. Light-weight clothing for the day and medium-weight for the evening in October.

- *November:* Pleasantly warm days. Medium-weight clothing with light woollies.

☐ MEDIA

(a) Newspapers

Cyprus has a large number of daily and weekly newspapers. "Cyprus Mail", the English newspaper, circulates as daily, while "Cyprus Weekly" circulates as weekly. However, nearly all English and other European newspapers and magazines are on sale, sometimes one day late.

(b) Radio

Radio channel 1 and channel 3 are in Greek while channel 2 transmits programmes in English, Turkish, Armenian and Arabic. It gives bulletins and forecasts of weather as well as music.

The English-speaking tourists can listen to the British Forces Broadcasting Service as well. There are also the BBC World Service programmes.

(c) Television

There are as many as seven channels that transmit colour material from the Cypriot T.V. Cyprus T.V. is linked with Greece and Eurovision for live transmission of Euronews as well as of special music, athletic events etc. The tourists will be able to watch a programme of their liking, even in their own language, in one of the seven canals.

Libraries

Pafos Municipal Library is open to public.
It is situated at Plateia Oktovriou 28, Pafos,
Tel: 26933847

Art Exhibitions, Galleries & Cultural Centres

Art Exhibitions are taking place almost continuously and the interested visitor is advised to make the necessary contacts with the galleries.

At the beach you only pay cash!

TBWA\ENTELIA

Kyklos, Tel: 26936681

Matisse, Tel: 26944973

Hellenic Bank Cultural Centre,
6, Nikodimou Mylona Str., 8047, Pafos,
Tel: 26815814

Kouklia Cultural Centre,
4, Michalaki Christodoulou Str., 8500,
Kouklia Village, Tel: 26432067

Popular Bank Educational Centre
10, Apostolou Pavlou Str., 8046, Pafos,
Tel: 26815814/26815861

❑ ELECTRICAL CURRENT-VOLTAGE

The electricity supply in Cyprus is 240 volts, 50 cycles A.C. Plugs are usually 5 amp or 13 amp, square-pin in most new buildings. Adaptors can be provided either by the hotel itself or by the local supermarket, grocery shop or electricians.

❑ CURRENCY

The currency of the Republic of Cyprus (as of Jan. 2008) is the Euro (€) which is divided into 100 cent. Notes in circulation are €500, €200, €100, €50, €20, €10 €5, while coins are €1 and €2 and 1, 2, 5, 10, 20 and 50 cent.

Credit and Debit cards

Credit cards can be used for cash withdrawals in local currency through ATMs located throughout Cyprus and in the arrivals area at Larnaka Airport.

Most of the hotels, shops and restaurants accept Credit Cards. Usually the Card symbol will be displayed in the shop-window or at the Reception.

Eurocheques and traveller's cheques are also accepted by all Banks and some shops and restaurants.

❑ POST SERVICES

Postage rates vary for different classes of mail and destinations.

Postage stamps may be purchased from: Post Offices, Hotels and News-stands or Kiosks.

Airmail Postage Rates (including refugee stamp):
- – To Europe and the Middle East:
  Letters not exceeding 20 grs: 53 cent
  Postcards: 45 cent
- – To USA, Africa and Far East:
  Letters not exceeding 20grs: 70 cent
  Postcards: 45 cent
- – To Australia and New Zealand:
  Letters not exceeding 20grs: 70 cent
  Postcards: 45 cent
- – Airletter to all countries: 45 cent

❑ EMERGENCY CALLS

In case of emergency, the tourist can telephone to the following numbers:

Ambulance	199/112
Fire service	199/112
Police	199/112
Night Pharmacies	11892
Hospitals:	
Lefkosia General Hospital	22603000
Lemesos General Hospital	25801100
Larnaka General Hospital	24800500
Paralimni Hospital	23200200
Pafos General Hospital	26803100
Polis Hospital	26821800

❑ METRIC CONVERSION

Since 1987 Cyprus jumped from the imperial system of weights and measures to the metric

Welcome
to our blue island!

Switch to Cytamobile-Vodafone for the Vodafone network in Cyprus and use your mobile just like at home!

Whether you have a postpaid or prepaid connection, you can call, text, send and receive picture messages and emails to share your holiday with your loved ones and work when you want to.

You can also use your familiar short codes to access your voicemail and customer care of your network, just like you do at home.

For more information please contact our Call Centre on 132 or visit our webpage at www.cytamobile-vodafone.com.

Cytamobile-Vodafone wishes you the best time here in Cyprus.

cytamobile

vodafone™

system. Temperatures are now given in degrees Celsius, petrol is sold by the litre, grocery items are sold in kilograms, fabric lengths are bought in metres and road distances or road speeds are posted in kilometres.

TIME IN TRAVELLER'S COUNTRY

At this particular moment, time in the following countries is either ahead or behind local Cyprus time as follows:

AHEAD	hours
Bahrain, Saudi Arabia,	
Iraq, Kuwait, Russian Fed (Variations)	1
Oman	2
India	3,30
China, Hong Kong	6
Japan	7
Australia	8
New Zealand	10
Syria, Algeria, Greece, Libya, Finland,	
Israel, Egypt, Lebanon, Bulgaria,	
Roumania, S. Africa	same
BEHIND	**hours**
Germany, Belgium, Denmark,	
Sweden, Austria, France, Italy,	
Spain, Switzerland, Norway,	
Netherlands, Poland, Hungary,	
Slovenia, Serbia	1
Marocco, U.K.	2
U.S.A., Canada	(variations) 7-10

USEFUL GREEK WORDS

The foreigner will find no difficulty in communicating with locals, since nearly everybody speaks or knows some English. Those in the tourist industry usually speak French, German, Italian as well as some other European languages, even probably Arabic. Some Greek words and phrases might be useful only in the village coffee shop and similar places where aged peasants may not know English. In an attempt to help the readers of this guide, we have selected a number of words and phrases which might be helpful to some tourists.

Alphabet

Αα	Alpha	short a
Ββ	Beta	v sound
Γγ	Gamma	g sound
Δδ	Delta	hard th
Εε	Epsilon	short e
Ζζ	Zita	z sound
Ηη	Eta	long e
Θθ	Theta	soft th
Ιι	Iota	short i
Κκ	Kappa	k sound
Λλ	Lambda	l sound
Μμ	Mi	m sound
Νν	Ni	n sound
Ξξ	Xi	x or ks sound
Οο	Omikron	short o
Ππ	Pi	p sound
Ρρ	Ro	r sound
Σσ	Sigma	s sound
Ττ	Taf	t sound
Υυ	Ipsilon	ee sound
Φφ	Phi	f sound
Χχ	Chi	guttural ch
Ψψ	Psi	ps
Ωω	Omega	Long o

Numbers

1	éna
2	dio
3	tria
4	téssera
5	pénde
6	éxi
7	epta
8	októ
9	ennia

10	déka
11	éndeka
12	dódeka
13	dekatria
14	dekatéssera
15	dekapénde
16	dekaéxi
17	dekaepta
18	dekaoktó
19	dekaennia
20	ikosi
30	trianda
40	saranda
50	peninda
100	ekató
101	ekatón éna
1000	chilia

Basic Vocabulary

good morning	Kaliméra
good evening	Kalispéra
goodnight	Kalinikta
good-bye	adio
hello	yasou
thank you	efcharistó
please/you are welcome	parakaló
yes/no	né/óchi
excuse me	sygnómi
where/when/how	pou/póte/pós
where is....?	pou ine?
how much is...?	póso kani?
I would like	tha ithela
How do you do?	ti kanete?
Fine, thank you	kala, efcharistó
Do you speak English?	milate anglika?
I don't speak Greek	den milo ellinika
Today/tomorrow/yesterday	simera/avrio/chtes
left/right	aristera/dexia
up/down	pano/kato
good/bad	kaló/kakó
here/there	edó/eki

now/after/before	tóra/meta/prin

Places

street	odós
avenue	leofóros
square	platia
restaurant	estiatório
hotel	xenodochio
post office	tachidromio
stamps	grammatósima
pharmacy	farmakio
doctor	yiatrós
hospital	nosokomio
bank	trapeza
police	astinomia
shop	katastima
petrol station	stathmós venzinis

Travelling

car	aftokinito
bus	leoforio
bus station	stasi ton leoforion
airport	aerodrómio
boat	plio
handbag	tsanda
wallet	portofóli
ticket	isitirio

Restaurant

food	fagitó
bread	psomi
lamb	arnaki
chicken	kotópoulo
meat balls	keftédes
meat on a skewer	souvlaki
water	neró
wine	krasi
beer	bira
coffee	kafé
milk	gala
refreshment	anapsiktikó

Days of the week

Sunday	Kyriaki
Monday	Deftéra
Tuesday	Triti
Wednesday	Tetarti
Thursday	Pempti
Friday	Paraskevi
Saturday	Savado

Shopping

sale	xepoulima
cheap/expensive	ftinó/akrivó
small/big	mikró/megalo
buy	agorazo
price	timi
colour	chróma
change	allazo
discount	ékptosi
clothes	roucha
bathing costume	mayió
how much is it?	póso kani?

Hotel

electric plug	priza
elevator	anelkistiras (ansanser)
pillow	maxilari
blanket	kouvérta
soap	sapouni
iron	sidero
key	klidi
room	domadio

– Do you have any available rooms..?
   échete adhia domatia?
– How much is the room per night..?
   possa kani to domadio yia kathe vrathi?
– I want a single/double room.
   thélo ena mono/diplo domatio
– Is there a T.V. set in the room?
   to domatio echi tileorasi?

INDEX

N

Galini
Varisela
Limnitis
Loutros
Xerovounos
Ammadies
Limmitis
Kampos
Tsakistra
E912
Kykkos Mon.
Mylikouri
958m
1318m
Cedar Valley Tomb of Makarios
Pano Panagia
Kato Pyrgos
Cape Kokkina
Pyrgos
Selemani (Agios Ioannis)
Pano Pyrgos
Frodisia
1362m
Tripylos (Cedars)
Stavros tis Psokas (Moufflon)
Agios Georgios Emmoni
Mansoura
Mosfili
Agios Theodoros
Challeri
Pigenia
TILLYRIA
Kaaouris
PAFOS FOREST
Agia Marogia
Kato Pyrgos
Pachyammos
Kokkina
Agio Giorgoudi
Selladi tou Appi
Livadi
Agyia
Kavravavou
Roisos ton skafon isle
Agios Rafail
Alevga
Paliampela
Xeros
746m
Makounta
Agios Merkourios
(see Stavros Nature Trails Map p.156)
Anadiou
Kiftou
Lasa
Livadi
Cape Pomos
Pomos
Nea Dimmata
Agia Marina
Gialia
Xeropotamos
Argaka
Kinousa
Pelathousa
Mirmikofou
Agios Isidoros
Steri
Lysos
Stavros tis Psokas
Melandra
Zacharia
Kios
Filousa
Saranta
Evretou
Loukrounou
Melaadela
Tremithousa
Peristerona
Skarfos Bridge
Simou
Embroidery
Fyti
Milia
Drymou
Lasa
CHRYSOCHOU BAY
Limni
Marion
Polis
(see Polis Street Map p.88)
Latsi
E713
Prodromi
Chrysochou
Karamoullides
Goudi
Cholli
Skoulli
Agia Akaterini
Kritou Tera
Pano Akourdalia
Kato Akourdalia
Agioi Anargyroi
Giolou
LAONA
E709
Fasli
Drouseia
Ineia
Kato Arodes
Pano Arodes
Androlikou
Pittokopos
Vlampouros
494m
Neo Chorio
428m
Smigies
Agios Georgios isle
Baths of Aphrodite
Fontana Amorosa
Chamili isle
(see Akamas Nature Trails Map p.128)
Mazaki isle
Cape Akamas
AKAMAS
Agios Konon
Geronisos isle
Lara
Lara Point
Turtle Hatchery